P9-CQI-780

Pelé

Pelé

James Buckley Jr.

DK PUBLISHING

LONDON, NEW YORK, MUNICH,
MELBOURNE, AND DELHI

Editor : John Searcy
Publishing Director : Beth Sutinis
Designer : Mark Johnson Davies
Art Director : Dirk Kaufman
Photo Research : Anne Burns Images
Production : Ivor Parker
DTP Designer : Kathy Farias

First American Edition, 2007

07 08 09 10 11 10 9 8 7 6 5 4 3 2 1
Published in the United States
by DK Publishing
375 Hudson Street
New York, New York 10014

DK books are available at special discounts
when purchased in bulk for sales
promotions, premiums, fund-raising,
or educational use. For details, contact:

DK Publishing Special Markets
375 Hudson Street
New York, New York 10014
SpecialSales@dk.com

A catalog record for this book is available
from the Library of Congress.

ISBN 978-0-7566-2987-8 (paperback)
ISBN 978-0-7566-2996-0 (hardcover)

Printed and bound in China
by South China Printing Co., Ltd.

Photography credits:
Front cover: Pictorial Press Ltd / Alamy
Back cover: POPPERFOTO / Alamy

Discover more at
www.dk.com

Contents

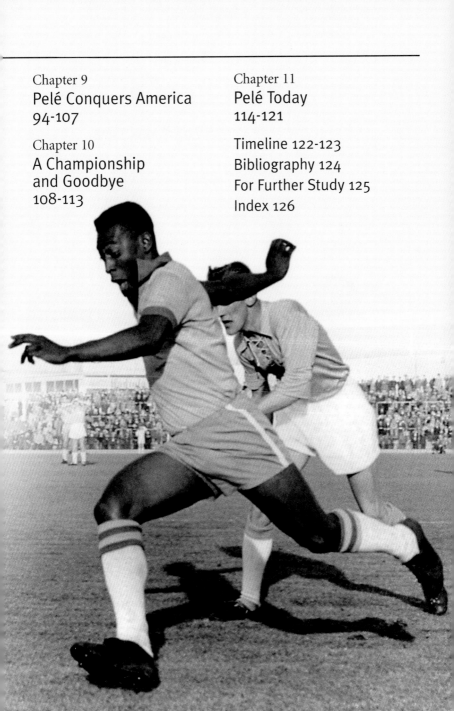

An End and a Beginning

On October 1, 1977, after the last game of the most glorious career in soccer history—perhaps in all of team sports history—a player known by only one name, Pelé, had to be carried off the field, shirtless and in tears. The shirt was not torn off in anger, but had become a souvenir. And Pelé was carried off not on a stretcher with an injury, but in triumph, on the shoulders of two teams. The tears, well . . . they were tears of joy. He waved tiny flags symbolizing the two countries—Brazil and the United States—that had embraced him for his skills, his love of the game, and his enthusiasm and joy.

Pelé enjoyed enormous popularity during his 22-year career, so he was used to being carried by crowds.

On that rainy evening in New Jersey, thousands of miles from the tiny Brazilian town where he had been born 37 years earlier, Pelé played his last game, leaving behind a legacy unmatched in sports. Soccer, the world's most popular game, is played, watched, and loved by literally billions of people. Today, 30 years after his final game, Pelé remains soccer's ultimate icon. He is the only man to be part of three World Cup championship teams—the man who brought soccer to America, who once stopped a war, who was named the Player of the Century in 2000. Kings have changed their schedules to meet him, presidents have juggled soccer balls with him. Even the worldwide fame of more recent sports icons like Michael Jordan or Tiger Woods pales when compared to the adoration Pelé enjoyed—and in some ways still enjoys. "How Do You Spell Pelé?" a newspaper headline once asked. The paper answered the question this way: "G–O–D."

As he rode above the cheering crowd that surrounded him that night, Pelé looked up into the dark sky, the rain mixing with his tears. What was he thinking as he made that final, triumphant ride? Perhaps he was looking back at the amazing road he had traveled to reach that day. A boy who had not owned a pair of shoes until he was seven years old had become, in a stunningly short time, one of the two or three most famous people in the world, his name a synonym for the world's game. What was Pelé thinking that day? Maybe he was thinking about all of this.

1

From Edson to Pelé

Until he was about seven or eight, Pelé was not Pelé. At birth, he was christened Edson Arantes do Nascimento, and that remains his real name today. (*Edson* came from the name of Thomas Edison, the American inventor, because electricity had only come to his village the year before.) However, it is a common Brazilian tradition for people to be known not by their birth name, but by a nickname. So, when João Ramos do Nascimento and his wife, Celeste, welcomed young Edson as their first born on October 23, 1940, in the little town of Tres Coraçoes, Brazil, they called him Dico (and many in his family continue to do so today). It wasn't until years later that Dico's friends gave him the name by which he became known to the world. Meanwhile, João Ramos himself was called Dondinho, and he was a soccer player, just like his son would grow up to be.

As shown here, Brazil takes up nearly half of South America. Most of the country's population lives in the south.

Dondinho had great hopes for his own soccer career, and at the time of Pelé's birth was moving up the ladder in the extensive network of Brazilian soccer clubs. In 1942, from the little club in Tres Coraçoes, he was invited to try out for a bigger club, Athletic Miniero. In his first game with them, however, he badly injured his knee; his dream of a long, successful career in the game he loved was over. Dondinho kept playing soccer for many years, but never at a level that brought in very much money.

When Pelé was four, Dondinho took a spot with a club in Bauru, a small town east of the giant mountains that shelter the interior of southern Brazil from the more prosperous coastal areas. The club would let Dondinho play for its number-one team and also get him a job in the city that would help him support his family. The money he would make playing

Why Pelé?

Although his every move was covered by cameras and reporters for more than 40 years, there is still one mystery about Pelé: Where did he get his nickname? Most of the Brazilian one-name soccer nicknames have some connection to the player's full name, or to where he is from, or what he looks like. But Pelé means nothing in Portuguese, the native language of Brazil, and to this day, Pelé himself is not sure where the name came from. In fact, he didn't like it at first, preferring the family's nickname of Dico. There are many theories of how the name came to be—a Turkish word, the mispronounced name of an earlier soccer star—but none are definitely true. It is, like the man who bears it, one of a kind . . . truly unique in the world.

soccer would simply not be enough. Unfortunately, this other job didn't come through, and the family struggled for several years. In his 1977 autobiography, Pelé wrote that, although the family didn't lack the basics—they had a home, a wood stove, an outhouse, and enough food— they suffered from constant worry about money and the problems it caused in the household. (And it was a crowded household, by then including Pelé's grandmother and uncle, along with his brother and sister.) He wrote: "Poverty is being robbed of self-respect and self-reliance. Poverty is fear." Pelé would go on in his career to earn millions upon millions of dollars, but he would always remember those feelings of fear. Money was not a driving force in his life, but it was always a concern (and his inexperience with it would cause him trouble later down the road). He knew that he was, for much of

What's in a Name?

In North America, we call Pelé's sport *soccer,* but in most other countries, it is called *football,* or some variation on that term (in Brazil, it is known as *futebol*). We, of course, use *football* to refer to a very different sport. As the two sports were evolving in the mid-1800s, American football became more popular in the United States, so it kept the name *football.* Pelé's sport, meanwhile, was called *association football.* The abbreviation for *association* was *assoc.,* which gave rise to the term *soccer.*

his career, one injury away from the life of Dondinho, forever struggling, forever wondering about "what might have been."

While his parents worked to keep the family together, Pelé played. He and his friends in Bauru played soccer at any time and any place they could. For poor boys like them, there were no soccer balls, nor cleats, nor even fields or goals. The ball

Pelé's mother, Celeste (right), always worried that he would go through the same soccer disappointment as his father, Dondinho (left).

they used was often just a big sock stuffed with rags or newspaper. The streets and empty lots were their fields, and Pelé and his younger brother Jair (always called by his nickname of Zoca) were part of a ragtag group of kids who played until the sun went down—or until their mothers called them home.

Pelé's mother, Celeste, was a big influence in his young life. The disappointment of Dondinho's short-circuited career would haunt her throughout her life. As Pelé moved his life toward a career in soccer, she resisted constantly, not wanting her boy to suffer the same pain and sadness that her husband had gone through. Pelé wrote that in his entire career, his mother never once watched an entire one

of his games live. She would watch highlights later, once she knew he was safe, but never in person. However, for all her objections, Pelé wanted to please her. "When Dona Celeste spoke, I obeyed," he wrote of his childhood in her house. (Later, Pelé would buy his parents a succession of houses, as he earned more and more money from his soccer career—certainly one way to ease his mother's fears!)

Although Pelé loved soccer, his first dreams were of a future in the air. A small, local airport and flying club attracted the youngster. He dreamed of zooming to romantic destinations "with the freedom of a bird." He wanted to fly away to make his fortune in a mythical happy place, and then return and take his family there, one by one, in his airplane. He later abandoned this dream almost overnight after watching through a dirty window as a coroner examined the mangled, bloodied body of a pilot who had crashed nearby.

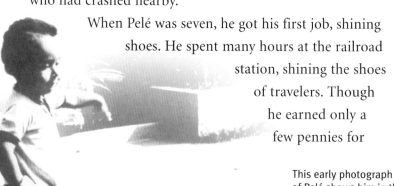

When Pelé was seven, he got his first job, shining shoes. He spent many hours at the railroad station, shining the shoes of travelers. Though he earned only a few pennies for

This early photograph of Pelé shows him in the act of ruining his nice new shoes by kicking a ball.

this work, it was enough to help his family. In his autobiography, he wrote of shining the boots of ranchers who brought their horses

D O N A

Dona is a Portuguese title that conveys respect. The male version is *Dom*.

into town to buy supplies, of airmen arriving to fly at the local club, of neighbors preparing for church on Sundays. It was with some of the money he earned doing this that Pelé was able to get his very first pair of shoes—he had gone barefoot all his life before then. The shoes were nice leather ones reserved for special occasions. Unfortunately, the soccer-crazy boy wore them to play once . . . and ruined them. "I just wanted to see how it felt to kick a ball with shoes on," he wrote.

About a year later, the long-promised job for Dondinho came through. He became an attendant at a local medical clinic, cleaning floors and changing sheets. Pelé would sometimes help out after leaving the railroad station. Together, they would talk about soccer and players that Dondinho had known and played against and about Pelé's dreams, first of flying and then of soccer. Pelé would later say that these evenings spent working together helped bring him closer to his father.

By this point, readers of Pelé's story are probably wondering, what about school? In a small town in Brazil at that time—the late 1940s—school was not automatic for every child. Many had to work or were destined for jobs that didn't need schooling, such as factory or farm work.

Nevertheless, Pelé's family wanted him to go to school. In the days when he still yearned for the air, they convinced him that a pilot needed to read maps and know about math to fly his plane. So, at the age of eight, he began attending the Brazilian equivalent of elementary school—a program that was supposed to last four years. And yes, he got to wear a pair of Sunday shoes when he went to school.

Unfortunately, school was never Pelé's favorite place to be, and the active boy struggled with the lessons, with sitting still, and with teachers telling him what to do. One punishment he endured for talking in class was having his cheeks stuffed with paper. Another was being made to kneel on hard, painful beans. Ultimately, Pelé would end up taking six years to complete the basic four years of school, and he would

Even today, young players in Brazil need only a street and a ball to play their national game.

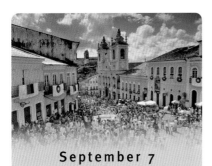

September 7

It's not unusual in South American and European cities to find streets named after dates, honoring events in the nation's history. In Brazil, September 7 is remembered as Independence Day, the day the nation became free of Portuguese colonial rule. Along with street names like September 7, an important legacy of that time is Brazil's national language, which remains Portuguese to this day.

not finish any higher education until more than 20 years later.

However, as a child, he would prove his intelligence and creativity in other ways. For example, he was the ringleader of a group of boys who formed their own neighborhood soccer team, naming it the September 7 Club after the street on which many of them lived. (Long after he became world famous, that same street was later named for Pelé himself.) It was also Pelé who came up with the idea of collecting all the soccer trading cards of Brazilian professional players and selling them in sets to fans. In this way, the boys could earn money to pay for uniforms. Another way they tried to earn money—not Pelé's idea, he wrote—was to steal peanuts from a warehouse to sell. After the theft, they hid the peanuts in a cave, but one sad day, there was a mudslide at the cave. All the boys got out, except one. This boy's body was dug out from beneath the mud soon after; it was a tragic event that Pelé never forgot.

The September 7 Club at first also called themselves "The Shoeless Ones," as they continued to play their games against other local teams in bare feet. However, they soon found out they were not the only shoeless team in town.

When Pelé was about 11, Zé Leite, a local businessman, saw the boys play and arranged for the Bauru Athletic Club to donate used soccer shoes to the team. Under a new name, Amériquinha, and with their first coach, Zé Leite himself, the team entered a citywide tournament for youth teams . . . and won! For the first time, the future international superstar heard the cheers of a crowd as he scored goal after goal.

Pelé went home joyfully carrying the 36 cruzeiros (the equivalent of a few dollars today) he had earned as part of the prize money.

This 1947 photo shows the poor quality of the fields that young Brazilian soccer teams had to play on.

Though he happily helped the family buy groceries with the money, his mother still didn't approve of his soccer exploits. She often saw her husband limping back from his games with Bauru Athletic Club's professional team and didn't want to see her son limp home someday, too. But talent like Pelé's could not be held back. In 1953, when he was 13, he took his first major step into the world of professional soccer: He was asked to join the Bauru Athletic Club's junior team. And he was introduced to a man who would change his life, former star player Waldemar de Brito. Pelé's life was about to kick into high gear.

The Kid Becomes a Star

To understand the road Pelé was about to travel, it's important to know how Brazilian soccer was organized at this time, the mid-1950s. There were no national youth leagues, such as today's AYSO in the United States, so those who wanted to play often had to form their own teams, as Pelé and his friends did. Most working parents had no time to coach the teams or run any sort of leagues, nor could they afford to bring snacks after the game or help teams sign up for photos. Instead, what existed were numerous athletic clubs, private organizations run by their members. These organizations

While Bauru didn't have large stadiums, cities such as São Paulo boasted sports palaces like this one.

sponsored several soccer teams each, from youth (approximate age levels: 12 to 15), junior (15 to 18), amateur (18 and up, but not yet professional), and professional, the top level. Players had to try out for each level and be asked to play; it was not as simple as just joining the club. The clubs would then arrange matches with other clubs, with the respective levels playing each other. Among the clubs, too, there were levels, with those in bigger cities often having the best players because they had more money to recruit athletes from other cities. Bauru Athletic Club (BAC) was made up mostly of players from Bauru, for example, as were most of the other clubs in the city.

Dondinho's connection with BAC made that club's owners look more closely at Pelé, and when they saw his success with Amériquinha, they invited him to join their club. "It was one of the most exciting days of my life," Pelé wrote. It was the first time that he got to wear soccer shoes that fit, play with a team that had regular practices and training, or benefit from the guidance of a real professional coach. The skills he had learned at the wounded knee of Dondinho and honed in the dusty streets with his friends could now be taken to a much higher level. In fact, if he kept playing with Bauru, he might soon play alongside his beloved father . . . if Dondinho's knee held out that long.

Pointing Pelé on the way to that next level was Waldemar de Brito, a former captain of Brazil's national team and one of the leading professional coaches of the day. To have him in charge of a junior team was like finding a former star for the

BICYCLE KICK

A bicycle kick is a difficult soccer move in which the player first kicks up one leg, then swings the other leg high over his head to hit the ball out of the air.

New York Yankees running a Little League baseball team. Pelé and his teammates were the lucky recipients of de Brito's wisdom. Pelé wrote that de Brito taught him many new things about the game, from dribbling techniques, to how to "bend" the ball, to the bicycle kick that Pelé would later make world-famous.

In just a short time, de Brito turned the boys of the streets into a formidable young team, winning several local tournaments. At this same time, Pelé was also playing indoor soccer, called in Portuguese *futebol de salao*, for another club. And he was

This photo, from later in his career, shows Pelé executing the crowd-pleasing bicycle kick.

The city of Rio de Janeiro is backed by a large mountain range; the largest peak is called Sugarloaf.

also working in a shoe factory attaching soles to boots, keeping his mother somewhat happy by having a life outside of soccer. The skills Pelé learned from de Brito and the goals he was scoring in matches with the youth and junior teams (he played for both) were attracting attention. Clubs in larger cities always kept their eye out for promising young talent in the small towns. Men like de Brito acted as scouts, too, letting big clubs know about potential stars.

When Pelé was 15, one of the teams from Rio de Janeiro, the nation's largest city and at the time its capital, sent a representative to Bauru to talk to Pelé about coming to play for their club, Bangú. Pelé was thrilled that such a big team would have interest in him, but Celeste put her foot down. In addition to her fears of crippling injury, she was also worried about her son being alone in such a big city. "Dico is only a baby," she cried. "Are you out of your mind, Dondinho? Dico go live in Rio? Alone? What nonsense!" That quickly ended the discussion of Rio. However, de Brito's experience told him that Pelé had the potential for great things. He knew that he would have to handle

Celeste carefully and help guide his young protégé to a club that would meet with her approval. He settled on Santos, located in a small coastal city of the same name, south of the city of São Paulo. After much discussion and even a long-distance phone call from the Santos president, it was decided that Pelé would be allowed to play for the club on a trial basis. (The call itself would have been a big event in those days in that part of Brazil . . . Pelé's family did not have their own phone and had to go to de Brito's hotel to take the call.)

Because of his youth and his family's financial circumstances, Pelé had always worn shorts up until this point. But now, wearing the first long pants of his life, he set off with his father on the train ride to his future.

Arriving at the Santos clubhouse, Pelé was awestruck. Here he was with men whose names he knew from the soccer cards, from

Pelé wrote of touching the sea for the first time on the beaches of Santos, on the Atlantic Ocean, south of São Paulo.

the radio, from newspaper stories. Here were some of the top professionals in the soccer-mad nation, and he was there in the locker room with them. "Welcome, Pelé," they said. "We've heard about you. Good to have you here." The little boy—he was still only 15, and weighed about 130 pounds—could only stare and mumble his answers. Dondinho, meanwhile, was greeted as an old friend. Pelé watched as Dondinho greeted former rivals like Zito, Jair, Formiga, Vasconcelos, and others.

Like all Brazilian clubs, Santos boasted passionate and noisy fans, here celebrating a 1961 win.

Pelé also met another man who would shape his future, a man known by one and all as Lula. Coach Luis Alonso had led Santos to the São Paulo state championship the year before and was regarded as one of the top club coaches in the country.

Santos, like most teams, had two or three different jerseys. In this 1959 game, Pelé wears the well-known Santos white.

"So you're the famous Pelé," he said upon meeting his future star. Soon after, de Brito and Dondinho left, and Pelé was alone, hundreds of miles from home, a boy among men. And he was homesick.

Many of the club's players lived in an apartment building, a kind of dormitory, called Vila Belmiro. Pelé lay in his bed in this building night after night and cried. Though he was training with the club's junior team, eating more food than he had ever seen in his life, and playing the game he loved, at times the distance from home got to him. Twice, he writes, he packed his bags and was heading to the railroad station to come home when a teammate or coach steered him back to the apartment or the field.

"I felt as if I was lost," he told *Sports Illustrated* in a 1966 article. "I was only 15 and suddenly I had to live with strange people in a strange place. I was afraid of failing, but even more I was afraid of the dark."

Growing up in the interior of the country, Pelé had never seen the ocean before he arrived at Santos. His first glimpse of it came from high above the hills to the east of the city,

as his bus wound back and forth along the road. Not long after arriving at the club, Pelé made his way to the beach for the first time. He walked in the warm sand, saw the stately seaside mansions (little did he know that he would one day own one), and tasted the ocean. As he had learned in school, it was indeed salty. Another new experience for the boy from Bauru.

Soon, the regular play and camaraderie with teammates helped Pelé overcome his homesickness. In fact, he temporarily picked up yet another nickname. The older players called him "Gasolina," because of the boundless energy he had on the field and off. They sent Gasolina on errands to get water or to pick up newspapers. He was becoming one of the guys.

Another Santos jersey featured vertical black and white stripes and a team-crest patch.

Meanwhile, on the field, he was quickly proving that he was more than just one of the guys. Not long after he arrived, he got to play in a "friendly" match with the Santos professional club. It was a stunning debut. Pelé scored four goals, his first ones ever in the black-and-white Santos jersey. Those goals didn't count toward his official

total, however. So, appropriately enough, it wasn't until September 7, 1956, that the former leader of the September 7 Club scored the first goal of what would become one of the highest-scoring careers in international soccer history. Against Corinthians, Pelé scored during a 7-1 victory. Goal number one. A stunning total of 1,280 would follow over the next 21 years. (In his 2006 autobiography, Pelé wrote that he later met the goalie who had let that ball slip through. The man had had cards printed up proudly announcing that he had given up the great Pelé's first career goal!)

Soon Pelé was not playing with the juniors anymore and was seeing more and more time with the professional-level team. Coach Lula saw that he had something special. He made sure that Pelé and Santos agreed on the young man's first full professional contract after he turned 16, the legal age for signing such documents. Pelé and

The Maracanã

If soccer in Brazil has a center, it's at the Maracanã in Rio de Janeiro. The proud holder of a Guinness World Record as the largest stadium of any kind in the world, the Maracanã, which opened in 1950, seats nearly 200,000 people in its concrete stands. It's an enormous ring that dominates its Rio neighborhood. Every world soccer fan has heard of the great games played at the fabled Maracanã.

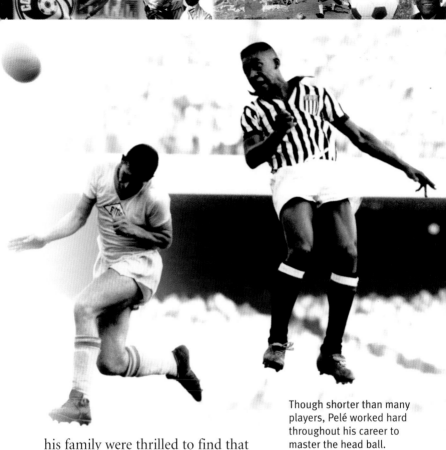

Though shorter than many players, Pelé worked hard throughout his career to master the head ball.

his family were thrilled to find that he was making about $75 a month, almost five times what Dondinho brought home from Bauru. Maybe this whole profesional soccer idea would work out after all.

With contract in hand, and his confidence building, Pelé really began to shine. The following summer, during a tournament at the Maracanã Stadium in Rio de Janeiro, he scored six goals in four games; he was the leading scorer, the *artilheiro*. Not long after, Pelé was chosen to play for the Brazilian national team. He was 16.

He was still a young man, however, and his mother still worried. Not long after his great performance in Rio, he left the team apartments and moved into a guest room at the home of Raimundo, a former basketball star. Raimundo's became a home-away-from-home for Pelé. No more dorm food, no more late nights up with the players. He was comfortable, well cared for, and, more importantly, his mother was pleased that he had a family to look after him.

Finally, in early 1958, Pelé was made happier than he had ever been. Though he had played for the national team in a tournament or two and he was the leading scorer in the São Paulo league in which Santos played, he was still only 17. The World Cup team that would represent Brazil was being chosen for that summer's tournament in Sweden. Pelé did

Pelé made his national team debut in 1957 wearing this jersey. In Portuguese, *Brazil* is spelled with an *s*.

Cup Teams and Club Teams

World Cup teams are not simply championship club teams, but all-star teams assembled from among the best players who are native to a country. Naturally, when making up those teams, the organizers look to the top club teams, so it was not surprising that many Santos players represented Brazil throughout Pelé's career. During World Cup qualifying games, as well as the actual competition, the players leave their clubs and play for the national team, returning to those clubs when their Cup duties are over. (A country's national team can also be assembled for other tournaments, so a player can be on the national team but not a World Cup team.) Being named to these teams is a great honor, of course, but also a lot of extra hard work. Imagine an NFL player leaving his team for a month in the middle of a season to play for a United States national team. It is a custom not really found in most other sports, but in soccer, clubs expect to frequently lose their top players.

not think he would be a part of it. He was too young, he thought. "I don't have enough experience," he said. But as he listened to the radio in his parents' home in Bauru, he still held out hope that he might be chosen.

The names of the chosen players were read one by one over the radio. And one of them was his. He was stunned. He couldn't speak. He couldn't even get out of his chair. His mother came in, and he managed to stammer out the news: "I've been chosen for the Brazil Selection [the official name of the team]."

His mother, however, was still not sure about soccer as a career. "Dico," she said, "let me feel your forehead. You don't look well."

chapter **3**

Attention, World: Meet the Future

Though Pelé reveled in being named to the Selection, his hard work was not over. The organizers of the team had invited more than 40 players to the tryout camp. Only 22 would travel to Sweden with the final World Cup team. In addition, there were no substitutions allowed during international games, back in those days. The 11 players who started a game finished it, unless they were too injured to return or were

The young Brazilian star drew media attention in Sweden as he prepared for his first World Cup.

The World Cup

The World Cup of soccer was first held in 1930 in Uruguay. Since then, the tournament, held every four years, has risen enormously in importance to its place today at the pinnacle of world sport. Its final game is far and away the most popular single-day sports event in the world. Billions of people watch every moment of the final, along with the dozens of games that lead up to it. When a country's team is playing, cities stop, schools let out, holidays are declared, business grinds to a halt. Even the Olympics doesn't get the glare of the World Cup; not every nation has a rooting interest in swimming or gymnastics. Almost every country, however, hopes to see its team hold up the World Cup trophy—the most coveted prize in sports.

PRIMER CAMPEONATO
MUNDIAL DE FOOTBALL
1924   1928
C   A
O   M
L   S
O   T
M   E
B   R
E   D
S   A
             M
1930 MONTEVIDEO
HOMENAJE A LOS
CAMPEONES MUNDIALES

1930 World Cup program

ejected for fouls. And even if a player left, he could not be replaced. So Pelé not only had to make the final 22, but hope that he might occasionally see action with the starting 11. As it would turn out, he saw more than just a little action.

The team played for several months in early 1958, training together and playing games against some of the regular Brazilian club teams. Pelé found himself more and more involved in the offense from his position as center forward. He was regularly getting starting spots, even in the place of older and more experienced players. However, when the day finally came to name the 22 who would go to Sweden, Pelé was nervous. In his autobiography, he tells of the team meeting at which the selections were announced.

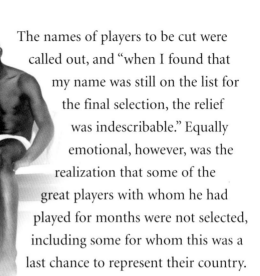

The names of players to be cut were called out, and "when I found that my name was still on the list for the final selection, the relief was indescribable." Equally emotional, however, was the realization that some of the great players with whom he had played for months were not selected, including some for whom this was a last chance to represent their country. The absence of one in particular— veteran striker Luisinho—caused a great uproar. In fact, the Selection was set to play against Luisinho and his team, Corinthians, not long after the selection was announced. Brazil's national team was actually booed before the game, so upset were the local fans about the snub of their hero. Nevertheless, Brazil beat Corinthians 3-1 and by the end, the crowd was cheering their country's team.

The sports medicine of 1958 was a far cry from today's; however, Pelé's doctors fixed him up in time to play.

Unfortunately, in that game, Pelé suffered a knee injury that threatened his trip to Sweden and would bother him off and on for years. In fact, he almost was not well enough to go with the team to Sweden. But he did the work and kept up his training, and when the team finally flew to Sweden for the World Cup in July, Pelé was on the plane. The youngster who had once dreamed of being a pilot was

on his very first airplane flight. Once he arrived, however, his knee injury and his youth kept him out of the lineup in Brazil's first two games, a victory over Austria and a scoreless tie with England.

While he bided his time on the bench during the matches, between games the 17-year-old enjoyed his first trip overseas. Sweden was a new world for Pelé, and he and his teammates saw the sights. Those sights included beautiful Swedish girls. Pelé had had girlfriends back in Brazil, but nothing serious. In Sweden, he met a young woman named Lena and spent time with her between games. The sights and sounds of a place so different from his home in Brazil thrilled the young man. But those sights and sounds faded when he saw that his

In Sweden, as in Brazil, Pelé's skin color didn't matter . . . only his amazing soccer skills.

Pelé relaxes with fellow superstars Didi and Garrincha between World Cup matches in Sweden.

name was in the starting lineup for the team's third game, against the Soviet Union.

As he trotted onto the field with his team, wearing his national colors in the sport's greatest competition, Pelé had a hard time realizing that his dream had come true. He had, in the space of just a few short years, made it from a tiny backwater town beyond the mountains to a place among the greatest players in the world. It was a mark of the greatness that he would bring to the sport, however, that he did not let his amazement get in the way of what he had come there to do: score and win.

Fellow forward Vavá scored the first goal for Brazil against the Soviet team. In the second half, Pelé made a perfect pass that Vavá put in the back of the net for a second

Wales

Wales is actually a part of the United Kingdom (it's in the southwest part of the main British isle) and not an independent country. However, because so many people in the UK play soccer, for many years, the world soccer authorities have let separate teams for Wales, Scotland, and Northern Ireland enter international competitions, along with a team from England itself.

goal. Brazil, in what was considered an upset, won the game 2-0. Pelé did not score, but that would change soon, as the greatest career in World Cup soccer history got underway.

Brazil's next opponent was Wales. Brazil had earned its place in this quarterfinal game by winning its four-team group. The top two teams from each of four groups advanced to the quarterfinals. While a team might have overcome a loss in the opening rounds, a loss in any game now would end a team's World Cup hopes. The Welsh team depended on stout defense and its huge, athletic goalie, Jack Kelsey. This strategy almost worked, as the creative and speedy Brazilian players were foiled time and again. After a scoreless first half, Brazil finally got its best chance midway through

A teammate hugs Pelé joyfully as the star dives into the net to recover his goal against Wales.

the second. Didi passed the ball in the air to Pelé, who was parked, as he often was, in front of the opponent's goal. Pelé let the ball bounce off his chest to his feet. In an amazing display of skill, he flicked the ball with his foot over the head of a Welsh defender, then turned and ran around the defender and blasted the ball toward the goal before it hit the ground. The volley caught Kelsey unaware and, although he dived, he couldn't stop the ball.

Goal, Brazil! Goal, Pelé!

The youngster ran to his teammates and leaped into their arms. The years of hard work, the hours in the street with a homemade ball, the nights of homesick crying in Santos, the pain that still throbbed in his

Before World Cup matches, both teams line up for the national anthems, as the Brazilian and French teams do here.

knee . . . all this and more flooded through his mind as the cheers of the crowd rained down on him. The game ended soon after; Pelé's goal had sent Brazil to the semifinals. At 17, he was the youngest player ever to play, let alone score, in a World Cup game.

The semifinal game would be against France, led by Just Fontaine. It was Brazil that struck first, as Vavá again took an assist from Pelé to score in only the second minute. France struck back soon after, as Fontaine beat Brazilian goalie Gilmar after a long dribbling run. Didi

Just Fontaine

After barely making the French team, forward Just [YOOST] Fontaine scored 13 goals in France's six games in the 1958 World Cup. That's still the all-time record for both a single World Cup and for career World Cup goals. Unfortunately, he broke his leg two years later and had to retire in 1961 after having scored 165 goals in 200 French league games.

then gave Brazil back the lead with a goal made after dribbling past several French defenders, and Brazil led 2-1 at the half.

In the second half, rather than rest on its lead and retreat into defense, Brazil kept attacking. The Brazilians' style of play—always advancing, using creative dribbling and amazing passes—was rare at the time. Soccer in those days was a bit more static. Teams played long balls and ran for

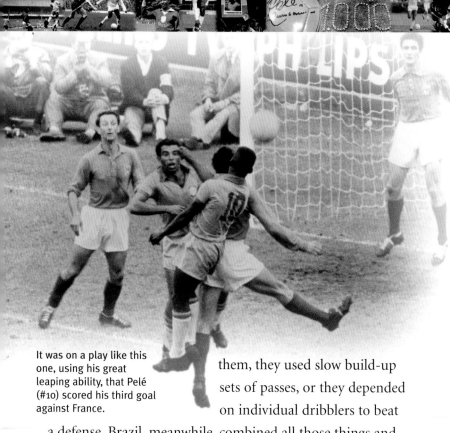

It was on a play like this one, using his great leaping ability, that Pelé (#10) scored his third goal against France.

them, they used slow build-up sets of passes, or they depended on individual dribblers to beat a defense. Brazil, meanwhile, combined all those things and added the flair of a South American samba beat. They played the sport many still call "the beautiful game" with flair and pizzazz. Staid European teams didn't know what to do with the flitting, flying, flashy forwards of Brazil.

Pelé scored a pair of goals in the second half, his second and third of the tournament. Both came off passes from Didi as the young forward zipped through the penalty area in front of the goal.

> **SAMBA**
>
> Samba is a popular type of music and dance from Brazil that has a bouncy beat. It's often played using drums and horns.

Pelé wasn't done, though, and during the game's final moments, as Brazil was focusing on keeping control of the ball and letting the clock tick down, Pelé struck again. Finding himself near the goal, he faced off against a French defender and scored his third point of the game: He flipped the ball over the man's head, ran around him, and one-timed the ball into the back of the net.

He was 17 and had scored a hat trick in a World Cup semifinal! It was unprecedented, it was amazing, it was the first act in a 20-year soccer spectacle that would play to cheering crowds around the world. The final was Brazil 5, France 2. Brazil, led by its amazing teenage scoring sensation, had earned a place in the World Cup final.

Sweden keeper Kalle Svennson is punching the ball, a typical way for goalies to clear a kick.

The last time Brazil had found itself in this position had come eight years earlier. In front of more than 200,000 people—mostly their fellow Brazilians—at the Maracanã Stadium, Brazil had lost in the 1950 World Cup final to Uruguay. It was one of the nation's most bitter sporting days, and every player on the

1958 team remembered that moment. They vowed that it would not happen again.

This time, they faced Sweden, who would play in front of its own home fans. The field was soaked after an overnight thunderstorm. Film of the game shows officials using giant sponges to soak up water from the wetter spots of the field. When the Swedes scored in the fourth minute, the crowd went wild. However, the experience and talent of Brazil came through. Vavá scored to tie it up and took a pass from Garrincha not long

It's a tough game: Pelé takes a breather after a collision in the epic 1958 World Cup final.

after to give Brazil a 2-1 halftime lead. Pelé then continued his amazing World Cup performance by scoring another stunning goal. Taking a long pass from Nilton Santos on his right thigh, he spun and hammered the ball with his left foot on a volley into the net.

And then . . . tears of joy. The former village kid hides his face among his teammates, overcome with emotion.

Later, Pelé described the aftermath of that first goal against Sweden: "I was screaming 'Goalllll!' and running and jumping in the air with a release of unbearable tension, and then I was being suffocated by my teammates swarming all over me . . . jumping on me from as far away as they could leap, wrapping their arms around my throat! But I didn't mind, I didn't even feel it."

A goal by Mário Zagallo brought the score to 4-1, seemingly sewing it up for Brazil, but Pelé was not finished. After Sweden got back one goal, Pelé put the final nail in the coffin. Using his powerful legs to leap above a Swedish defender, he nodded the ball with his head into a high arc that rose, untouchable, into the far upper corner of the net. It was his second goal of the game, his sixth of the tournament, and it was a thing of beauty. "After he scored that one," Swedish goalie Sigge Parling later said, "I felt like applauding."

Brazil's 4-2-4

In 1958, Brazil debuted a formation that sparked a soccer revolution. They sported four forwards, two midfielders, and four defenders in front of the goalkeeper. This formation called for players who knew each other and each others' moves intimately. It also called for both "selfish" dribbling skills and unselfish, precise passing. Prior to the 4-2-4, teams often had five forwards, but that left only two defenders in the back, which led to high-scoring shootouts. The 4-2-4 created balance between offense and defense, while leaving room for creativity and attack. As result of Brazil's success, teams soon began playing more and more players in the backfield and defense became more important than offense. Today, there are often only one or two forwards or "strikers."

The whistle blew shortly after and Brazil was the World Cup champion for the first time. Pelé was carried off the field by his teammates, his face awash in tears of joy, his expression one of an emotional, overwhelmed boy rather than a hardened pro.

Fans streamed onto the field. The Brazilian players danced and hugged. They carried giant Brazilian flags around the field. Sweden's King Gustav came to award them their medals and the Jules Rimet Trophy, reserved for the winner of the World Cup tournament. One reporter called the play of the Brazilians "a dazzling display of football wizardry." The team's five goals were the most ever in a World Cup final.

In just a few games, Pelé had gone from a near-nobody to one of the most famous soccer players in the world. In the coming days, he would learn a bit more about what that fame meant. It turned out that being a World Cup champion

meant that everyone back in Brazil thought he belonged to them. It was more than a week before Pelé could make it back home to Bauru to see his family. First there was a parade in Rio, a meeting with the country's president, another parade and a big welcome-home dinner in São Paulo, then numerous events and parties in Santos. It was almost too much for Pelé and he was grateful to finally arrive in Bauru. After one more

Pelé and Sweden's Adolf Gustav VI meet before the 1958 World Cup final.

parade around the cheering town, he could finally settle down. He slept in his own bed, in his own home, but he was no

The victorious 1958 Brazilian World Cup team poses with the Jules Rimet trophy.

longer the little boy of the streets . . .
he belonged to the world now.

chapter 4

A National Treasure

If Pelé thought the week after the World Cup had been a whirlwind of activity, it turned out to be just the start of the busiest couple of years of his life. Though he was now a World Cup champion and the national team's top scoring threat, he was also still an employee of Santos. He returned to the club soon after the victory parties ended. Wanting to take advantage of its players' successes—Santos had sent three other players along with Pelé to the World Cup— the club made up a grueling schedule.

The two-level city of Salvador was one of the many places in Brazil that Pelé's newfound fame let him explore.

First up was a tour of Brazil itself. Along with playing its regular games in the São Paulo state league, Santos headed to big cities like Rio de Janeiro, Recife, and Porto Alegre. Although he had enjoyed his travels in Sweden, Pelé's trips around his native country were almost as eye-opening. Brazil is a large country with a great variety of environments. Rio is a mighty city by the ocean, while Curitiba is in the middle of a huge forest. Salvador is built on two levels and connected by

Following the World Cup, it was back to Santos for Pelé. The club would soon take advantage of his fame.

tramways and elevators. Seeing more of his country—and loving all of it—helped turn Pelé into a real ambassador. For the rest of his life, he has continued to promote Brazil around the world during his travels.

In early 1959, Pelé and Santos played 14 games in six weeks during a tour of Central and South America. As it played the top local clubs, as well as visiting European teams like Czechoslovakia, the team was on the road constantly. It was tiring work, but Santos won 13 of the games. There was no rest for Pelé when the tour was over, however, as the São Paulo state team then played in a countrywide tournament. (The state team was an all-star team chosen from teams in São Paulo.)

Pelé had been playing nonstop since early 1958, but there was no break yet for the young superstar. Up next was another trip to Europe. There Santos played the top clubs in several countries on a schedule designed, as Pelé described it, to make money for Santos without worrying about the impact on the players. But regardless of his feelings, Pelé was an employee and had to do what the bosses wanted. This was the first of several times in his career that he would express unhappiness with the Brazilian soccer system. The biggest game on the European tour was against Spanish giant Real Madrid. With Pelé on its side, Santos was regarded as among the world's best teams. Real Madrid, however, felt it owned that title—it had dominated Spanish and European play for years. The matchup happened in late 1959, at the end of Santos' grueling European trip— and the Brazilians lost 5-3. It was a disappointment to Pelé, but he knew that if his

Real Madrid

Real [RAY-ahl] Madrid of Spain is perhaps the most successful and famous soccer club of all time. The team has won 29 championships of La Liga, the Spanish league, 9 European club championships, and 3 world club titles, along with just about every major tournament in Europe. Its famous all-white uniforms have become synonymous with top-flight soccer. In 2000, FIFA, the world soccer organizing body, named Real Madrid the top club of the 20th century. Over the decades, its success and wealth have allowed the club to sign up some of the greatest players of all time, among them such superstars as Alfredo di Stefano, Luis Figo, Ferenc Puskás, and David Beckham.

team had not been tired and had players missing due to injury, Santos would have won.

An exhausted Pelé came home after that trip having completed an amazing year. He had played 44 games with Santos. The team's record was 31–8–5. All together, including state team play, Pelé had scored 126 goals in 82 games, by far his highest total in a single year.

Even today, Pelé's autograph, whether on a ball or elsewhere, is one of the most sought-after among collectors.

Pelé had also reached another total that year: his 18th year. At that time in Brazil, all young men had to serve a year in the army when they turned 18— no exceptions for superstar soccer players. In fact, the army was happy to have Pelé, who was immediately made part of its own soccer team. Because the army also occasionally released him to play for the national squad, he was, in late 1959 and early 1960, playing for five different teams: Santos, Brazil, the state all-star team, his army base team, and the Brazilian army national team . . . all at the same time!

It was thus a bit of relief to finish his army time in 1960 and get back to focusing on Santos. The club's European success led to another tour, this time a joint trip with the Brazilian national team. The first part of the tour saw Pelé playing only for the national team. He enjoyed the leisurely

schedule—about three games every two weeks. He got to see the pyramids in Egypt, the ancient buildings of Rome, and a return to Sweden (where the team trounced top club Malmo 7-1). About three weeks later, Pelé's workload doubled as Santos played games in France, Italy, and Denmark.

Returning to Brazil, Pelé continued to play for Santos and remained its leading scoring threat. One of the goals in 1959 came in a game against Italian club Juventus in São Paulo. He flipped the ball over two defenders, dove between them, and headed the ball into the goal; he remembered it in 1966 as "my best goal, from a technical

Returning to the scene of his first international triumph, Pelé scored two goals in a 1960 win over a Swedish club.

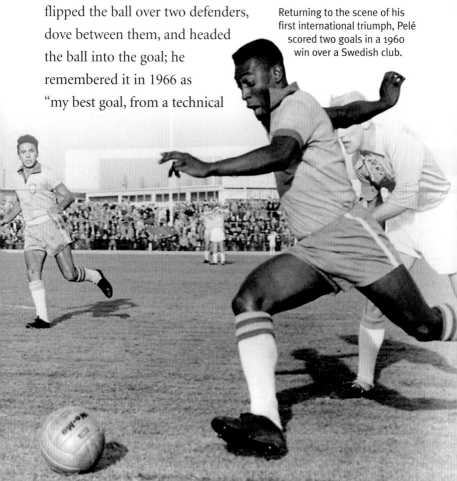

standpoint." However, in early 1961, playing
for Santos at the great Maracanã Stadium
against the club Fluminense of Rio, Pelé
scored what others call his greatest
goal. Indeed, it is still talked about in
Brazil four decades later. Taking the
ball in his own penalty area, he
dribbled through the nine members
of the Fluminense team, never passing
once. Finally, as the enormous crowd's
screams rose, Pelé finished off this
amazing run by scoring past a hapless
goalie. It was such a stupendous goal
that a plaque was put up at the
stadium declaring it the greatest goal ever scored there.

Pelé receives
treatment for an
injury in a 1961 game
with Santos.

While the goals and victories kept coming, there were two
other very important developments in Pelé's life off the field.
Both would have repercussions for many years, some good,
some not so good.

First, in 1958, fresh from his World Cup coming-out
party, Pelé met a young women named Rosemari. He first
spotted her when he and some teammates, looking for
something to do one evening,
went to see a girls'
basketball game played by
another part of the Santos
sports club. As they watched

PENALTY AREA

The penalty area is the only
place on the field where a
goalie can only use his hands.
Serious fouls inside this area
result in a penalty kick.

Pelé and the Popes

In 1961, during another European tour, Pelé got to meet with Pope John XXIII. As a lifelong and very devout Catholic, this was a special honor for Pelé. Several years later, he would meet with Pope Paul VI (it was said at the time that the pope was more nervous about meeting Pelé than Pelé was about meeting the pope). Pelé also met with Pope John Paul II, a former soccer player himself, and later Pope Benedict XVI. They were just four of the dozens of world leaders that Pelé met thanks to his soccer skills and generous personality.

the game, Pelé watched only one girl: Rosemari.

He tracked her down through other club members and went to meet her at the record store where she worked. It turned out that she had noticed him, too, though Pelé would worry for years that she and others liked him just for being famous, not for just being, well, plain old Edson.

At the time they met, he was only 17, and she was only 14, so in a conservative country like Brazil dating was not possible. But he was smitten and arranged to "visit" her family often. Supervised by her parents or her aunt, Rosemari could spend time with the soccer star, though there was no talk of a "serious" relationship. Pelé and Rosemari would continue to see each other this way for several years.

The other relationship that Pelé started around this time was with a local businessman named Jose Gonzales Osoris, known as Pepe Gordo. By 1960, Pelé was earning what would today be nearly a million dollars in salary from Santos, and more from endorsing products. However, his lack of

schooling and experience meant that he had little idea what to do with all this money. Through a teammate, Pelé met Pepe Gordo and hired him to help arrange his business affairs. Pelé, having seen what had happened to his father, knew that his sports career could end in an instant with one bad injury. He wanted to make sure that he would have money even after his soccer life was over. Pepe Gordo and Pelé bought a large store and several other businesses. Pelé then turned his attention back to the field (and to Rosemari), leaving the business details to Pepe Gordo. It would prove to be one of the worst decisions of his life.

Amid all of this, Pele got one piece of good news: His success meant that clubs around the world wanted to add him to their rosters. Huge amounts of money were offered, including as much as $500,000 from an Italian club. However, knowing how important the young player was to Brazil, the country took an unusual step. President Janio Quadros issued a ruling that Pelé was a "national treasure," and could therefore not be exported legally. Pelé, for his part, was perfectly happy playing only, as he said, "for Brazil, for São Paulo, and for Santos."

The playful hold Pepe Gordo has on Pelé would have been put to better use on Pelé's finances.

Championships, Heartbreaks, and Love

If the years leading up to Pelé's second World Cup appearance in 1962 were busy, the year 1962 itself was one filled with championships.

Brazil had earned an automatic bid to the World Cup as the defending champion. This meant they did not have to play the long series of qualifying matches that all the other teams (except host Chile) would have to play. Brazil had a chance to prepare without pressure. The only thing they had to worry about was a serious injury. Unfortunately, that's just what happened to Pelé.

During a pre-tournament friendly game against Portugal, Pelé felt a sharp pull in his upper leg. He

Mário Zagallo, far left in this photo of members of the 1962 team, would later become Pelé's national team coach.

finished the match, but doctors found out afterward that he had badly strained his left groin muscle. This muscle, on the inside of the thigh, is very important to a soccer player. Of course, the legs power the player and the feet kick the ball, but the groin muscles come into play frequently as a player stops, starts, turns, and moves. Pelé was in great pain, but kept playing, scoring a goal in each of the final pre-tournament games.

CAMPEONATO MUNDIAL DE FUTBOL
WORLD FOOTBALL CHAMPIONSHIP
CHAMPIONNAT MONDIAL DE FOOTBALL
COUPE JULES RIMET

CHILE 1962

The World Cup returned to South America for the third time in 1962. Uruguay had been the host in 1930, followed by Brazil in 1950.

At the World Cup in Chile, things started out as expected for both Brazil and its star, who had added another nickname or two; in the press, Pelé was now sometimes called "The Black Pearl" and *"O Rei,"* which means simply "the king." In the first game, Brazil beat Mexico 2-0, with Pelé scoring one of the goals. Early in the next game, against Czechoslovakia, Pelé took a hard shot that hit the post. As it did, Pelé hit the ground. He had aggravated his groin injury and could barely walk. He was helped off the field, but

GROIN MUSCLES

The groin muscles extend along the inside of each leg from the lower pelvis to the knee. You can feel them by pressing along the top of your inner thigh.

since he could not be replaced in the lineup, he hobbled back in. Even at half-strength, Pelé had to be guarded, and did what he could to help. Later, in

his 1977 autobiography, Pelé gave credit for sportsmanship to the Czech defenders who could easily have tackled him hard and put him out of the game for good. "While they protected the interest of their team," he wrote, "they also protected me." This sort of treatment would start to disappear in the years ahead, however.

Brazil ended up tying the game 0-0, but the bad news was that Pelé was out, probably for the rest of the

This was not the outfit that Pelé wanted to be wearing, but he put on a brave face as he watched from the stands.

tournament. After watching from his bed as Brazil beat Spain and from the stands as they defeated Chile in the semifinals, Pelé still thought he might recover enough to come back for the final. But two days before that game, he reinjured his groin during warm-ups. He was out of the World Cup.

"Watching from the stands hurt more than my groin," he wrote. However, he watched with a smile as his teammates beat Czechoslovakia 3-1 to win its second straight World Cup. Pelé was thrilled, of course, but worried that his place with the team might be threatened.

After returning home, he continued playing for Santos. He recovered from his injury and led his club team to a series of international triumphs and the greatest single season in its

history. First, they captured the championship in the Copa Libertadores, the championship of all South America, in which the finest clubs of the entire soccer-mad continent played in a long tournament. The final was a three-game playoff against Peñarol of Uruguay. After winning the first of the three games, Santos was shocked in its home stadium and lost to Peñarol. However, in the clinching game, played in Buenos Aires, Santos won 3-0.

Vavá leaps to celebrate the third and game-clinching goal by Brazil in their 1962 World Cup final win over Czechoslovakia.

Eusébio

Eusébio da Silva Ferreira was perhaps Portugal's finest player ever. Born in the colony of Mozambique, he helped Portugal win the European Cup in 1962 and was the top scorer in the 1966 World Cup. In league play, he was twice the leading scorer in Europe and was the continent's 1966 player of the year. He retired in 1974 due to an injury, having scored 727 goals in 715 games.

After this, more victories quickly followed. Soon, having captured the São Paulo championship and the South American title, Santos set its sights on the world. The 1959 tour by Santos had sparked the creation of a new international tournament among the top clubs: the Intercontinental Cup, or World Club Championship. Over the course of the entire summer, with time off for the World Cup, the top clubs in the world played off against each other. Amid all this amazing soccer talent, Pelé once again rose above the crowd. He was the top scorer in the event, with 52 goals, and led Santos into the two-game final against Benfica of Portugal and its star player, Eusébio, who rivaled even Pelé in terms of stature and skill.

In the first final at the Maracanã, Pelé scored once and Santos won 3-2. In the second game, Pelé went to new heights, scoring three times—a hat trick—in Santos' 5-2 victory.

The mighty Santos team, sporting eight players who were among Brazil's 22 national-team players, continued its success in 1963, repeating as Copa Libertadores winner and picking up its second straight Intercontinental Cup. The club continued its fine play through 1964, winning another São Paulo championship and taking additional tours of South America.

The next big events in Pelé's life were almost completely opposite in nature. First, there was the joy of finally getting engaged to Rosemari. In his autobiography, he tells the story of asking for her hand in marriage in the summer of 1965. Ironically, the man who had played in front of hundreds of thousands of people, who had met kings and popes and presidents, who was the hero to millions around the world . . . was nervous! He went fishing with Rosemari's dad, Guilherme, and gently brought up the subject of marriage. Guilherme didn't seem surprised. After all, Pelé had been coming around their house for years, even as he became an international star. But the older man didn't give an answer, so Pelé had to sit in the boat for hours waiting until they could go home and Guilherme could talk it over with his wife.

Famous visitors to Brazil got to meet the country's most famous person; here Pelé visits with U.S. senator Robert Kennedy.

By wearing their club jerseys, World Cup teammates Pelé and Vavá show that they are still rivals in the club world.

Everyone, including Rosemari, said yes, and the marriage was planned for early in 1966. However, a dark cloud would hang over the event, thanks—or no thanks—to Pepe Gordo. Not long before the wedding day, Pepe Gordo came to report bad news: Pelé was out of money. The companies that Pepe Gordo had set up had all lost money or gone out of business. A series of very bad choices by Pepe Gordo and his associates had caused Pelé's earnings from soccer and endorsements to essentially vanish. What was worse, the men had taken out loans on Pelé's behalf that were now due. Pelé was in serious financial trouble.

A 1966 article in *Sports Illustrated* described a scene that foreshadowed Pelé's troubles. After watching Pelé halfheartedly sign papers and checks with Pepe Gordo, the writer observed that Pelé "approached the duties of business with none of the enthusiasm he shows on the playing field." Pelé's inattention to the businesses was as much a part of the problem as Pepe Gordo's poor decisions. Though he had given Pepe Gordo all his trust, it was still Pelé's job to make sure that trust was

earned. However it happened, the young man who had known poverty as a youth but for whom money remained a mystery found himself in need

of help. He got it from a familiar source: Santos. The club arranged to loan him the money to cover his debts as part of a new contract. As a result, Pelé would end up playing for most of an entire season for no pay. But, as he wrote, it was better than the alternative of going into bankruptcy.

A more happy event that year was his marriage to Rosemari. Like a celebrity wedding today, it was covered intensely in the Brazilian press, for

Although rarely nervous on the field, Pelé had to check his perspiration during his 1966 wedding to Rosemari.

whom Pelé remained a godlike figure. Photographers scrambled around Pelé's large house to try to get photos of the private ceremony. Rumors swirled around the event, including one that the marriage would be held at the Maracanã in Rio because so many people wanted to come. Instead, Pelé and Rosemari limited the guests to a few family members, friends, and teammates.

The couple traveled around Europe on their honeymoon, with Pelé enjoying visits with people and players he had met on earlier trips there. He took Rosemari to meet Pope Paul VI, they

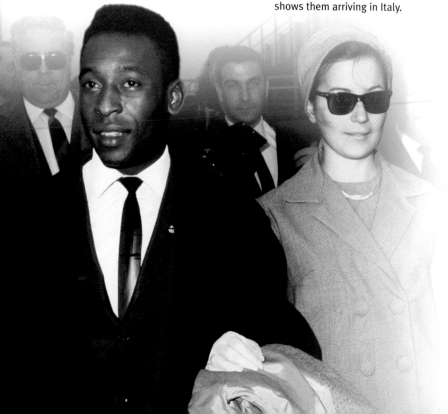

The world followed Pelé and Rosemari on their honeymoon. This snapshot shows them arriving in Italy.

For a Catholic couple like Rosemari and Pelé, getting to meet their church's leader was a special treat.

enjoyed a special reception at the magnificent town hall in Vienna, they toured the German and Italian Alps, and they explored the streets of France. For the little boy from Bauru, it was heaven—he was in a wonderful land with the woman he had loved for years finally at his side.

But the roller coaster that was 1966 took another downward swing when the Brazilian team gathered once again to attempt the impossible: win three straight World Cups. The event that year was held in England, and Pelé was a marked man. As the dashing and brilliant play of Brazil had evolved over his time with the team, more and more teams had resorted to harsh tactics to stop him. That was the case in England in one of the sport's ugliest moments.

Pelé was uncomfortable with the 1966 Brazilian team from the beginning. The organizers, he felt, had not chosen the team in the best way and had not selected the right coaches. Instead of keeping the main 22 players together for pre-tournament training, they divided them up and played them in different places. Thus, the team did not have its usual unity, a key part of their style of play. Pelé also felt that the

team was not as physically prepared as they should have been. Pelé and his veteran teammates went to England and would play, but they were not happy.

Pelé was even more unhappy after the team's first game, against Bulgaria. Although Brazil won 2-0, and Pelé scored a goal on a free kick, the Bulgarian defenders had hacked and kicked at Pelé so much that his legs were aching. Unable to stop him fairly, they had resorted to simply fouling him whenever he got the ball. Then, in another sign of disorganization, the managers unbelievably chose to leave Pelé out of the lineup against Hungary . . . and Brazil lost 3-1. It was the first World Cup loss by the team in 12 years. Then, adding to the confusion among the players, the coaches made

Here, a Hungarian player uses an illegal two-footed tackle on Pelé. Some thought it was the only way to stop him.

seven lineup changes for their third game, against Portugal and the mighty Eusébio.

Pelé was almost literally mauled on the field. An official FIFA video of the 1966 World Cup calls it "one of the most shameful acts in soccer history." A succession of

Moments after the play shown on the opposite page, an injured Pelé was helped off the field for treatment.

Portuguese defenders, notably João Morais, simply kicked and struck Pelé. Fans at the game were screaming for justice, but none came from the referee, who many suspected was trying to help the hometown English team avoid the Brazilians down the line. Pelé was finally taken out with a vicious two-footed tackle that injured his already sore knee. He was out of the game. Soon after, so was Brazil, defeated 3-1 and eliminated from the final round.

"I am not sad at defeat," Pelé said after the games, "only that I have not been allowed to play soccer. Ideal soccer has become impossible. This is terrible for the game and for the spectators who want to see a show."

Not long after the World Cup ended in England (with England winning over West Germany in the final), Pelé and Santos hit the road again, this time on Pelé's first trip to North America. The short trip,

TACKLE

In soccer, a tackle is a defensive move in which a player slides at ground level into the path of the player with the ball, in an effort to knock the ball away.

Yankee Stadium is known as the "House that Ruth Built," after the New York Yankees' famous slugger Babe Ruth.

covered mostly by local journalists who couldn't understand what all the fuss was about, showed the state of soccer in the United States—namely, that to see any great soccer there, it had to come from somewhere else. There was no real soccer league in the country; the game barely registered. That would all change, thanks to Pelé, but not for another decade or more.

In August 1966, a three-team mini-tournament had been set up between Santos, Benfica, and AEK of Greece. The games would all be played in New York City. A single game would later be played between Santos and famed Italian club Inter Milan at Yankee Stadium.

Santos won the mini-tournament by defeating Benfica 3-2, in a game that saw goals by both Pelé and Eusébio. The games were played at a tiny stadium on an island in New York's East River and attended almost entirely by immigrant citizens longing for a taste of their favorite sport from back home.

Against Inter Milan, Pelé scored Santos' third goal in a 4-1 victory. The 41,000-plus spectators at the game made up the largest crowd to see a soccer game in the United States in more than 40 years. (Even in this game, noted the *New York Times*, Pelé was "tripped, mauled, kneed, and elbowed.") That attendance record was one that Pelé would help break again and again in the years to come.

So, as 1966 ended, Pelé looked back at a year in which he had lost all his money, gotten married, and, for the first time since 1958, made a disappointing return from the World Cup. As the year ended, he vowed never to play in another World Cup for Brazil. Fortunately for Brazil and soccer fans around the world, he would later forget that vow in order to achieve the greatest soccer triumph of his career.

Pelé waves to cars in front of the famous Macy's department store in New York's Herald Square.

chapter **6**

On the Road and in the Record Books

Before the next World Cup would come four more years of soccer with Pelé's beloved Santos. The championships in Brazil continued, as Santos dominated São Paulo state play, while also winning numerous small tournaments in South America. However, the world titles were not coming anymore, as club teams around the world had improved to match and exceed its talents. Nevertheless, Santos remained among the most popular clubs, and the team still went on international tours every year.

For a person so devoted to family, the birth of his first child, Kelly Cristina, made life complete for Pelé.

For Kelly, the trophies and medals won by her famous dad were just shiny toys.

Meanwhile, in 1967, a joyous event occurred in the life of Pelé and Rosemari: the birth of their daughter Kelly. As Santos arranged more and more tours for their team and its famous star, Pelé came to see that leaving a family behind to travel made soccer more difficult and the trips seem longer. However, he wrote in his 2006 autobiography, having Kelly helped his play. "It was impossible not to shrug off the pressures [of work and business] when I was around her, and it really helped me rediscover my love of the game."

A 1967 South American tour was followed by another trip to Europe and then to Africa. Pelé wrote about this African trip extensively in both of his autobiographies. He and his club were thronged wherever they went, drawing enormous crowds at every game and appearance. "Everywhere I went I was looked upon and treated as a god," he wrote, "almost certainly because I represented to the blacks in those countries what a black man could accomplish in a country where there was little racial prejudice, as well as providing physical evidence that a black man could become rich, even in a white man's country."

67

Though not yet a household name in the United States, Pelé still drew big crowds, such as at this 1968 game in Washington, D.C.

For Pelé, the issue of race was present only on the edges of his life. In multicultural Brazil, he faced none of the hardships that blacks in America suffered during the same period. He was beloved regardless of his skin color or heritage. He really only came up against the issue in a strong way after marrying Rosemari, who was white. It had not really occurred to him that it would be an issue until people, especially in other countries, started asking about it. Throughout his life, Pelé would speak out against racism, but thanks to his country's attitudes toward race, he only rarely faced its ugly specter in person.

On his second trip to the United States in 1968, Pelé saw a hint of his future. Along with a trip to New York, Santos played in Cleveland, Washington, D.C., Boston, and other cities. Pelé saw that he was somewhat better known than he had been on his first trip, and that soccer had begun to carve out a tiny foothold in the United States. "I came to realize that America was a vast reservoir for future soccer," he wrote.

The year before, articles appeared saying that U.S. teams would try to convince Pelé to come and play for an

American club. Although this actually happened almost a decade later, it seemed unthinkable at the time. In the mid-1960s, Pelé coming to play soccer in the United States would have been like superstar baseball player Albert Pujols leaving the St. Louis Cardinals to play first base for a team in Iceland. It would make no sense at all. Just to be sure, though, Pelé told reporters, "Not even for all the money in the world would I leave Brazil or Santos." Eventually, it would not take all the money in the world . . . just a lot of it.

In early 1969, the ever-active Brazilian press did some figuring and concluded that Pelé might

Showing the drive that made him such a great scorer, Pelé muscles past an Oakland defender in a 1968 game.

Pelé Stops a War

Perhaps the most famous international tour event in Pelé's amazing career came in 1969. Santos was scheduled to play club teams in the African nation of Congo. However, a civil war was raging in the nation. Both sides wanted so badly to see Pelé play that they literally stopped fighting for two days. The Pelé Truce in January of that year meant that Santos got a chance to play one match in Kinshasa and two in Brazzaville (they had to "lose" the second game in order to get out safely!). Sadly, the truce lasted only until Pelé left . . . and then fighting resumed.

have a chance to score the 1,000th goal of his career that year, if he kept up his pace of 40 to 50 goals per year. As the numbers grew, the anticipation of the big event grew even faster. Game by game, the papers and fans counted up to the magic number. Only two other players in soccer history had reached that total, and they had played in the very early days of the sport, when the game was more high-scoring and the talent levels not nearly as equal. Plus, of course, everyone felt that it was right that the mighty Pele "own" this remarkable record.

The count went on through the fall, and on November 12, 1969, he scored two goals against Santa Cruz, taking him up to 998 for his career. Then, he scored one more in the next game, against the Botafogo club, in the town of João Pessoa, capital of the little state of Paraíba. As it turned out, there was plenty of time left in that game for Pelé to score one more goal, and the local fans became ecstatic at the thought that the magic total would be reached in their

A Brazilian postage stamp honored Pelé's 1,000th goal.

hometown. However, the Santos goalkeeper fell very ill not long after number 999 and, believe it or not, Pelé was the team's reserve goalkeeper. So, as the fans jeered in anger, Pelé moved back to play goalie for the rest of the match. There would be no goal 1,000 in João Pessoa. In any case, many Brazilian fans hoped that he would reach that total at a much larger stadium. The next game was at Bahia, a venue people felt appropriate for the occasion, but Pelé could only hit the crossbar and the fans there went away disappointed as well.

What a moment: Pelé rises above the crowd, holding up the ball he used to score his historic 1,000th goal.

Finally, on November 19, Santos faced a club called Vasco de Gama, in a game at the Maracanã. Amid a driving rainstorm, the place was packed with fans eager to see something really special, and this time the other team helped make it happen. Midway through the second half, Pelé was driving toward a clean shot on a goal when he was fouled by the defender Fernando. The referee's whistle of a foul was drowned out by the cheers of the crowd who knew what would happen next: a penalty kick.

These special kicks, made from 12 yards (11 meters) out with only the goalie to defend against them, almost always result in a goal. Pelé, of course, stepped up to take the kick. Shaking off some

In celebration of his 1,000th goal, Pelé stands next to the lucky number, written entirely in soccer balls.

nerves, he whacked the ball into the right corner of the net. The crowd erupted with cheers as Pelé ran into the goal to grab the ball. People poured onto the field to celebrate his a1,000th goal. His jersey was ripped from his back. Pelé jogged around the entire field, waving to the cheering crowd, followed by packs of fans and photographers. Someone handed him another jersey, this one with some added numbers; his famous number 10 now read "1000."

To go along with his success on the field, Pelé was now doing better off the field as well. Another adviser, named Marby Ramundini, had straightened out his finances. Ramundini—whom Pelé would watch more carefully than Pepe Gordo—also took a more active role in promoting Pelé. He arranged

In 1962, a Brazilian company briefly produced this Pelé-themed liquor, but stopped when the star objected.

for higher fees for Pelé to promote products. "Ramundini taught me never to underestimate the power of a well-known and respected name," wrote a modest and humble Pelé, who had to be pushed into using his fame to make money. He did, however, continue his lifelong policy of never endorsing any alcohol or tobacco products.

Soon, the celebration for the goal faded, and as Brazil gathered its forces for the 1970 World Cup, eager to avenge its 1966 disappointment, everyone wondered just one thing: Would Pelé play?

Brazil, Brazil, Brazil!

Disappointment over Brazil's losses and the way the team had been managed in 1966 had left Pelé with a very bad taste in his mouth, to go along with the pain in his legs. He had not been happy with the organizers, he had been left out of one game for no reason, and then he had been hacked on the field by opponents. All of these were factors in his famous declaration that he would not play in another World Cup.

But as Brazil began to form its team for the 1970 World Cup, to be held in Mexico, Pelé slowly changed his mind.

Pelé's former teammate, Mário Zagallo, coached perhaps the finest team ever to win the World Cup.

Part of the reason was that the coach would be Mário Zagallo, who had been his teammate during the 1958 and 1962 World Cups. He respected Zagallo and knew that the players would get fair treatment and good preparation. In the end, Pelé decided to come back for his fourth World Cup tournament, becoming the first player ever to appear in four World Cups. Also, if Brazil could win its third world title, it would take permanent possession of the Jules Rimet Trophy. Three titles

meant that the winning nation "owned" the trophy—a redesigned trophy would be created to take its place.

Arriving in Mexico, Pelé found himself in the middle of an unusual media swirl. Along with the regular crowds of reporters asking about the game and the team, there were others asking about Pelé's eyes. A rumor had been started—Pelé thought by a bitter João Saldanha, who had been the national team coach before Zagallo took over—that the superstar suffered from myopia, a condition that narrowed his vision and could impact his play. Pelé insisted there was nothing wrong with him, but the rumor dominated the talk before Brazil's first game.

With a third championship, Brazil would "own" this Jules Rimet trophy.

The gossip swirled, the press clamored, Brazil's fans fretted, but once that first game began, Pelé forgot it all and just played. Here on the field, he could escape all the off-field problems and controversies and just do what he loved most: play soccer.

The opponent was Czechoslovakia, and the Czechs put the Brazilians on edge by scoring just 11 minutes into the game. After a tying free-kick goal by Rivelino, Pelé came close to scoring perhaps the most remarkable goal in World Cup history. As it was, it remains one of the highlights of his amazing career, even though the ball didn't go in! He had

noticed that the Czech goalie, Ivo Viktor, ranged far out of his goal box when the play was far upfield. Late in the first half, Pelé got the ball at just about the midfield mark. Without pausing, he hit a high, arcing shot toward the goal, and over the out-of-position Viktor's head. The crowd gasped as the ball curved slowly toward the net . . . and then barely missed, sailing just outside the left post. It was nearly a miraculous 65-yard (50-meter) shot—in a World Cup game, no less. Wrote Pelé: "So much for myopia!"

In the second half, Brazil scored three times to put the game away. Pelé got a point himself on a wonderful goal, taking a high pass on his chest and then kicking it in off the volley. The final score was 4-1, Brazil. Next up was defending World Cup champion England.

As has been seen, the Brazilian style of play was exciting to watch, a samba

English goalie Gordon Banks is just about to land after denying Pelé a goal with one of the most famous saves in World Cup history.

dance of movement, creativity, and speed. The Brazilians attacked first and defended second. The English players, on the other hand, did the opposite, focusing on keeping the opponents out of the goal area and preventing goals. They usually scored on counterattacks or after long kicks from the back. When the teams—the most recent two World Cup champs— went head to head, it was a contrast of styles. The soccer world waited to see which

Gordon Banks

Though he is best known for that single save, Gordon Banks has more on his résumé than that. For 10 years, he was the goalkeeper for England's national team, helping his country win its only World Cup, in 1966. England lost only nine of the 73 games he started for them, and he remains on the list of the all-time great goalies.

would prevail. Zagallo, however, had a trick up his sleeve. Instead of attacking, the Brazilians surprised everyone by playing in the British style. They didn't attack in waves, they held some forwards back on defense, and the result was a scoreless first half.

There was nearly one goal and it was another signature moment for Pelé—again on a goal he didn't score. On a high pass from Jairzinho, Pelé leaped and headed what looked like a sure goal at the lower corner of the English net. In a flash, the English goalie, Gordon Banks, leaped almost across the

entire goal to barely tip the ball around the post. It remains to this day perhaps the most famous save by a goalie in World Cup history.

One reason that this play, Pelé's long near-miss, and the entire 1970 World Cup in general are so well remembered more than 30 years later can be explained in two letters: TV. For the first time, the World Cup was broadcast live, worldwide, and in color. More than one billion people tuned in to watch. They saw it live, but billions more have seen highlights in the years since. Although only those present saw some of Pelé's early goals in Brazil, such as the "goal of the plaque" in 1961, everyone could see for themselves just how great he was now that he was captured on film.

Beginning a soccer tradition, England's Bobby Moore and Brazil's Pelé exchange jerseys after their World Cup game.

Those same fans also saw Pelé show off another of his wondrous skills to help Brazil score the only goal of the England game. After his teammate Tostão gave him a perfect pass, Pelé drew the defense to himself. His opponents fully expected him to make the shot, and he let them believe. Then, at the last second,

Peru goalie Luis Rubiños (right) can only watch helplessly as the great Jairzinho moves in to score.

before they could stop him, he flicked the ball instead to an unguarded Jairzinho, who completed the goal. Brazil led and held on to win 1-0. Zagallo's tactics had worked; of course, it helped when he had players of Pelé and Jairzinho's class.

Brazil made it into the quarterfinals with a 3-2 victory over Romania, as Pelé added two more goals to his ever-increasing total. The first came on a stunning, swerving free kick that bent like a banana around the Romanian defense to slam into the far side of the net. The second came as he slid full-out to nudge in a rebound at the far post.

Next up, against Peru, he didn't score but had a great time. "The game itself was a joy to play in," he wrote. "It was attack followed by attack from both sides." Part of the reason was

that Peru played the same style as Brazil, with an emphasis on offense. Indeed, they were coached by Didi, another former teammate of Pelé's from the Brazilian team. Pelé had an assist off a deflected shot and Tostão had two goals as Brazil was back to the semifinals with a 4-2 victory.

Pelé writes that the team filed into the locker room after this game and, without changing or showering, gathered around the radio to hear the result of the other quarterfinal: the Soviet Union versus Uruguay. Brazil would play the winner, and to a man, they were all pulling for one result. In overtime came the answer they wanted: Uruguay 1-0.

Why did Brazil want to play their fellow South Americans? Turn back the clock 20 years to find out. That was the year, 1950, that Uruguay defeated Brazil in the World Cup final . . . and to

Still a bitter memory for many, this 1950 goal by Uruguay crushed Brazil's hopes of winning the World Cup at home.

make the defeat more painful, they did so in the Maracaña, in front of Brazil's home fans. Pelé remembered seeing his father cry for the first time when that game

SOFT GOAL

A soft goal is one that is either hit softly, is mis-hit or, should probably have been stopped, as opposed to a hard shot aimed at a particular part of the goal.

came over the radio in their home in Bauru. No one in Brazil, certainly not its best players, would ever forget that moment. Pelé claims that he vowed that day to avenge the loss when he grew up. There's no way to know if this story is really true, but it's part of his legend now—and, vow or no vow, this game against Brazil's old nemesis was the chance the entire country had been waiting for. Pelé writes that dozens of Brazilians, from reporters to officials to fans, gave him one message: "You can lose the championship, but do not lose to Uruguay!"

Things almost got away from Brazil as they gave up a soft goal early in the first half. Only a late goal by Clodoaldo sent them to halftime tied 1-1. The first half of this game also included yet another near-miss by Pelé that has taken on legendary status. Racing toward a pefect through ball, Pelé faked out the goalkeeper by jumping, so that the goalie dove to his right at his legs. The only problem—for the goalie—was that Pelé had let the ball go past the goalie's left. Pelé skipped over the keeper's hands, ran on to the ball, and then just missed the empty goal from a tough angle. Basically, he faked out the goalie without ever touching the ball.

THROUGH BALL

A through ball is a pass that cuts between defenders so that an offensive player can run past them to catch up to the ball.

In the second half, Brazil's constant attacks, along with the players' determination, put them ahead to stay. Jairzinho scored first and then Pelé assisted on a third goal. The 1950 defeat was forgotten. Uruguay was behind them and ahead lay only one team between Brazil and World Cup immortality: Italy.

Bicycle kicks can be defensive, too. Here an Italian defender uses the challenging move to try to clear the ball.

Italy, like England, focused on defense. Their defense was called *catenaccio* in Italian, meaning "door bolt." They literally tried to lock up the goal. As Pelé points out in his 2006 book, however, Brazil just "created too much pressure." The attacking skills of the Brazilians overran the solid defense of the Italians.

More than one billion people watched on TV while Mexico City's Azteca Stadium was filled with more than 100,000 people. In the back of his mind, Pelé probably knew that this would be his last World Cup game, so it was definitely the right moment to have what he would later call "one of my best games in a Brazil shirt."

In fact, Pelé scored the first goal of the game. It came on a header (a goal scored with the head), as he outleaped a taller defender to hammer the ball past the goalie. The enduring

image of this World Cup, and perhaps Pelé's entire career, came immediately after that goal. Pelé scored and than ran up the field. He leaped into the arms of his teammate Rivelino and pumped his right arm and fist in the air. His yelling, smiling, beaming, joyous face was seen by people the world over. Those who had only read about Pelé or seen occasional photos or short films could now see him in living color. If you watch the clip, he looks like the little boy who was still rejoicing with his September 7 teammates after a victory over a club from across town in Bauru. He is the youngster who thrilled the world at 17. Although he is playing in his last World Cup game, he still expresses the sheer joy of the game that he has come to represent. And it was thanks to TV that so many around the world shared that moment and could see it again and again over the years.

Following that celebration, Italy tied the game with a goal caused by a Brazilian mistake. In the second half, however, Brazil's attack continued. Gérson scored only a few minutes into the half and Jairzinho followed with a hard shot that found the back of the net. With that goal, he set a record by being the first player to score in every game of a single World Cup tournament.

Pelé celebrates during the final match with Italy, which he would later call "one of my best games in a Brazil shirt."

With the game in hand, Brazil continued to celebrate soccer by attacking, passing, dribbling, and showing the world how the game could be played. Many experts regard this 1970 Brazil team as one of the best, if not *the* best, overall World Cup team of all time. Fittingly, Pelé assisted on the game's final goal,

Pelé's teammates hoist him onto their shoulders after Brazil's third World Cup win.

drawing the defense to himself (as he had in the England game) and then slotting a pass right onto the feet of an onrushing Carlos Alberto, whose powerful, unstoppable, right-footed shot was the exclamation point on Brazil's overwhelming 4-1 win.

Brazil had done it: They were the first three-time World Cup champions. Team captain Carlos Alberto raised the trophy high to the crowd in Mexico City, and the Jules Rimet Trophy became forever Brazilian. Pelé, too, had set a record as the first man to be part of three World Cup–winning teams; he was the only link to Brazil's two earlier triumphs. It seemed no matter what teammates he played with, he could use his amazing skills to lead them to victory.

Jules Rimet

Until Brazil took it home for keeps in 1970, the trophy given to the World Cup champion was named for Jules Rimet, who was the president of the French football federation and later president of FIFA until 1954. Rimet was instrumental in organizing the first World Cup competition, in 1930.

Pelé had scored four goals in the six games, wrapping up the most brilliant World Cup career ever. Though his 12 career World Cup goals (in 14 games) are not the all-time record, his goals were among the most entertaining, the most creative, and the most meaningful. The little boy from Bauru had become the greatest in the world.

What had made him so good for so long? A quote from 1975 explains it in Pelé's own words:

> You need balance and speed and strength. But there is something else that God has given me. It's an extra instinct for the game. Sometimes I can take the ball and no one can foresee any danger. And then two or three seconds later, there is a goal. This doesn't make me proud, it makes me humble, because it is a talent that God gave me.

By tradition, the winning team captain—here it's Carlos Alberto—receives the World Cup trophy from the host nation's leader.

Throughout his life, Pelé has always given credit for his success to God and his Catholic faith—and the successes kept coming. With the Cup behind him, at the age of only 29, what other worlds were left for his talents to conquer?

chapter 8

What's Next?

Pelé's joy over winning his third World Cup was joined not long after the team returned home by the joy of the birth of his son. He had actually left the team's post-Mexico celebrations early to return to see Rosemari. In his 1977 book, he expressed dismay that the press criticized him for going back so quickly, while the team continued its series of parades, dinners, and celebrations. Still, he wrote that he knew that the people of Brazil thought he had done the right thing, "because each of them would do the same."

Pelé and Rosemari named their son Edson Cholbi Nascimento and he was nicknamed Edinho. So Pelé found himself with two young children and a wife at home who wanted and needed his attention, combined with a job that, at the moment, demanded almost constant travel. Something had to change.

First, however, he took time during the next season with Santos

Pelé talks with his son during a break in training, in 1977. Edinho was seven years old at the time the picture was taken.

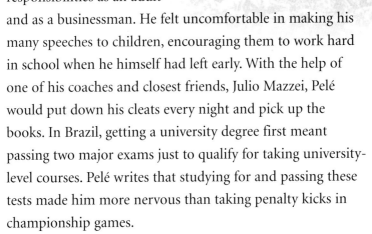

Pelé wrote that he found greatest peace on his farm in Brazil, where he loved to play music.

to do something he had not done since he was a small boy in Bauru: go to school. Pelé felt that his education was too limited for his many responsibilities as an adult and as a businessman. He felt uncomfortable in making his many speeches to children, encouraging them to work hard in school when he himself had left early. With the help of one of his coaches and closest friends, Julio Mazzei, Pelé would put down his cleats every night and pick up the books. In Brazil, getting a university degree first meant passing two major exams just to qualify for taking university-level courses. Pelé writes that studying for and passing these tests made him more nervous than taking penalty kicks in championship games.

But pass them he did (though he almost failed the swimming test!) and he soon enrolled at the university in Santos. Superstar or not, he was expected to be at the all-day classes and to be on time. He was even subjected to the typical teasing and hazing given to all freshman (including his first close-shave haircut). Finally, he proudly finished all

the necessary classwork and would one day show his children that he was a college graduate.

Back on the field, Pelé was making other changes in his life. A year after the World Cup triumph in Mexico, he decided to leave the Brazil national team once and for all. He wanted to leave that team at the top of his skills, not after they declined as he got older.

During his last game for Brazil, Pelé ran a lap of honor, jogging around the entire stadium as fans cheered.

Plus, he didn't want to have to travel the world and be away from his family for the next World Cup. "I had been in four World Cups," he wrote. "It is enough."

After a long tour through Central and South America, Pelé knew it was time to take off the bright-yellow jersey for the final time. On July 18, 1971, in a game against Yugoslavia before 180,000 people in the Maracanã, the greatest international player of all time played his final international game. Following the 2-2 tie, Pelé ran around the entire field as the Brazilian fans cried and chanted, *"Fica! Fica!"* which means "Stay! Stay!" Pelé was in tears, too, but he stuck by his decision.

During that final tour, while the Brazilian team was in Jamaica, Pelé met a man who would soon have a huge impact on his career—and on soccer. Clive Toye was the president of the New York Cosmos, a team in the six-year-old North

American Soccer League. Compared to even the smallest Brazilian club, the Cosmos were tiny. Yet there was Toye, introducing himself and talking to Pelé and Julio Mazzei about having Pelé come to New York to play. It was a crazy idea. If Pelé would not leave Brazil to play for Real Madrid or a top Italian club, he certainly would not leave for a team that played on a dirt field in a small college stadium before fewer than 1,000 fans a game. However, the incident stuck with Pelé and would eventually change his life.

Another event from this time would also lead to big things down the road, though at the time, Pelé was heavily criticized for it. While talking with Santos about a new contract, he used his celebrity and fame to take a stand.

Though his national-team career was over, Pelé remained a hero to millions of Brazilians.

At the time, Brazilian soccer players had very few rights. They were essentially bound to their clubs for life, making it very hard for them to change teams or make their own choices. They were also left unprotected by Brazil's many laws designed to improve the lives of workers, such as those that provided health care, pensions, and job security. Pelé and other top players began a campaign to change this. Because this would have been a big change for soccer in Brazil, many people were angry at Pelé for trying to force it. When something has been a certain way for many years, change, even for the better, is seen as a threat. Eventually, Pelé agreed to two more years, one for pay and a portion of overseas games money, and another for which the club would donate his salary to charity.

On another tour with Santos, in 1973, Pelé returned to the United States. During a game in Baltimore, he scored directly on a corner kick for the only time in his career. On this same tour, he met Henry Kissinger, the country's national security

advisor, who would later play a small but important role in Pelé's life. During that tour, Kissinger was helping his

CORNER KICK

A corner kick occurs when the offensive team returns an out-of-bounds ball to play by kicking it from the corner of the field.

friend João Havelange earn a new job as president of FIFA. Eventually, the Brazilian Havelange would get the job and run world soccer for decades.

By 1974, after 18 years of continuous play, Pelé was nearing the end of his career with Santos. While he worried about how to make that separation finally happen, and what it would mean, he traveled to West Germany to watch Brazil play in the 1974 World Cup. Many fans wanted him to play, but he stuck to his decision and watched from the stands. He still met with the players, however, and encouraged them. He also worked for Brazilian radio and television, and for a British newspaper, commenting on the games.

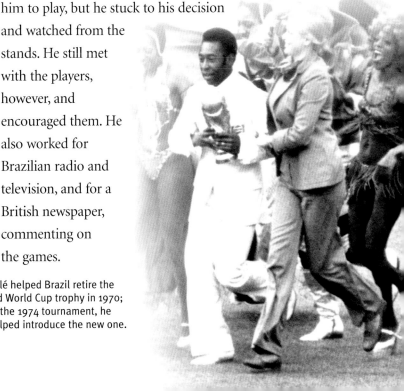

Pelé helped Brazil retire the old World Cup trophy in 1970; at the 1974 tournament, he helped introduce the new one.

Johan Cruyff

Johan Cruyff [CROYF] was seen by many as the "next Pelé" in the early 1970s. He led Ajax Amsterdam to a World Club championship and seven Dutch league titles, along with three European Cups. He was the first truly all-around soccer superstar, as good on offense as he was on defense. Led by Cruyff, Holland perfected the idea of "Total Football," in which every player could play every position (except goalie).

Without Pelé, Brazil still did fairly well, making it to the semifinals. However, the team lacked its usual flair and tied twice in the early rounds. In the semifinal, they were defeated by Holland and their great midfielder Johan Cruyff. Instead of Brazil earning its fourth title, there would be a new World Cup champion this year, host West Germany.

Finally, it was time for the biggest change in Pelé's life so far. It was time to leave Santos. He had helped them win the 1973 state championship, and had been the leading scorer again. But his contract was up and he had other things on his mind. He wanted to leave the game he loved while he was still physically fit and uninjured. After a long buildup by the club (during which they advertised several games as Pelé's "last" to draw in crowds), the end came on October 2, 1974. As he had with so many events throughout his career, Pelé crafted the end of

his Brazilian soccer life in a memorable, one-of-a-kind way. About 20 minutes into the game, he suddenly caught the ball in midair . . . with his hands! Later, he described this farewell in detail:

I ran with the ball to the center of the field, placed it on the center spot, and knelt, my knees on either side of the ball, and raised my arms in a cross to face the fans, turning from side to side so that all could see. The tears were running down my cheeks without control.

Pelé stood and took off his shirt and waved it to the crowd who stood and cheered for many minutes until finally he left the field. Little did anyone know at that time that he would be back on the field in just over a year and playing in the last place anyone would have expected.

As Pelé waved goodbye to fans in his last match for Santos, he probably couldn't imagine the worlds he would go on to conquer.

Pelé Conquers America

Not long after Pelé left Santos and turned to what he thought would be a businessman's life, "in at nine and home by five," another financial problem ended that dream. A large company that he owned part of, Fiolax, could not pay back a loan and was also hit with fines by the Brazilian government for some illegal business dealings. Pelé, after yet more bad advice, was found to be responsible for these payments, totaling more than $2 million. All of a sudden, he was a man without a regular job and with an enormous debt.

In a search of a way to make a lot of money fast, Pelé realized his best chance was to return to the soccer field. The only question was where. The meeting with Clive Toye back in Jamaica made him think that U.S. soccer might be the answer.

Although Pelé tried to remodel himself as a businessman, he was generally more at home on the field.

However, in the mid-1970s, American soccer was still a very low-profile sport. The American Youth Soccer Organization (AYSO), today more than 12 million strong, was a decade old, but

EDSON ARANTES DO NASCIMENTO
DIRETOR

American soccer in the 1970s was a far cry from the artful game played by teams in other countries.

only a hint of what it would later become. The North American Soccer League (NASL) was the only professional soccer league. It was nine years old but smaller than America's indoor lacrosse league is today (yes, there is an indoor lacrosse league). The league's players all had regular jobs that they worked during and after the seasons. The games were played in tiny stadiums before even tinier crowds. It was so far below the radar of the American sports scene that it barely registered. However, it had one thing going for it: Steve Ross.

Steve Ross

Steve Ross had his hand in just about every entertainment pie in America in the 1970s. Under his guidance, Warner helped popularize cable TV and video games, made dozens of movies, helped sell many popular music acts, and ran DC Comics. Ross merged Warner with media giant Time Inc. in a $14 billion deal in 1989. He passed away in 1992.

Ross, an entertainment mogul and head of Warner Communications, saw the NASL as a way to own a sports team, which he had always wanted to do. He started the New York Cosmos in 1968 and brought in former British soccer coach and official Clive Toye to run it. Though they won the league title in 1972, the Cosmos were struggling to gain fans and the league was losing teams left and right. Ross, from his background in the movie and TV businesses, knew that big stars brought big crowds. He told Toye to find the biggest star he could to play for the Cosmos. That star was Pelé, of course, and Toye again contacted Pelé's associate, Julio Mazzei, with an offer that was perfectly timed. Pelé needed a team, a big splash, and a lot of money. Ross and the Cosmos were the ones who could give it to him.

But before the actual offers of money came in, Mazzei and Pelé made up two lists to decide if this was the right move.

By this time, Mazzei had evolved from trainer and coach to personal advisor; Pelé called him "Professor" or even "Daddy." Together, the pair made one list of 17 negatives and another with 18 positives. Some of the negatives included the fact that people in Brazil might dislike him for leaving them behind, the fact that the Brazilian government might not let him go, and even the issue of his being a black athlete in a nation with a long history of racism. On the positive side, of course, was the money, which would surely be enough to pay off his debts and set him up for life. Plus, making his name famous in the world's biggest market would mean even more money down the road. And there was the chance to bring the game he loved to a new country. Rosemari wanted to see what life would be like in America and looked forward to an American education for their children. It was an enormous decision, but after consulting with his family, Mazzei, and others, Pelé made the call: Let's go to America.

It was largely the determination and effort of Clive Toye that led to Pelé coming to America.

As Pelé himself has written, the next step in this process is worth almost a book in itself. Bringing Pelé to the United States involved dozens of people, lawyers

in two countries, thousands of miles on airplanes, hundreds of hours of long-distance phone calls, and even the vice president of the United States.

Toye led the talks with Pelé, playing to the Brazilian star's love of the game. As Toye said in *Once in a Lifetime,* a 2006 documentary about the Cosmos, "I told Pelé, 'You could go to Juventus or Real Madrid and you can win another championship. Or you can come to America and win a country.'"

Back and forth went the plane rides, the contract offers, and the lawyers. The money offered rose up and up until finally, Pelé accepted. Exactly what the final contract was is a subject of some debate. Published reports, Toye, Warner officials, and the Cosmos all offer slightly different totals, ranging from $2.7 million to $7 million. The probable truth is somewhere in the middle; *Sports Illustrated* uses the figure of $4.5 million as the total package, as Pelé agreed not only to play for the Cosmos for three years, but also to be represented in marketing deals by Warner for 10 years and even to work with Warner's music arm to make records. That doesn't sound like much money

Teacher, trainer, advisor, friend: Former Brazilian official Julio Mazzei played many roles in Pelé's life.

today, when even ordinary athletes earn several times that amount for just one year, but in those days, it was a stunning fortune. Baseball's highest-paid player, home-run king Hank Aaron, earned $200,000 that year, and suddenly here was a man in a sport few Americans cared about earning 20 times as much. As Pelé noted in his 1977 book, it was more money than he had earned by playing 18 years for Santos. It was a bold move by Ross and the Cosmos.

Henry Kissinger

Henry Kissinger went from being a German-born professor at Harvard to one of the most important public figures in the world. He was the U.S. secretary of state from 1973 to 1977 and played a huge role in American foreign policy before and after his time in that job. In 1973, he won the Nobel Peace Prize for his help with Arab-Israeli peace talks. He also was awarded the Presidential Medal of Freedom.

Even that money was not enough, however. One final step remained: getting Brazil to let go of Pelé, the country's soccer-playing "national treasure." First, Warner executives contacted U.S. vice president Nelson Rockefeller, whose family owned Rockefeller Center, where Warner had its New York City headquarters. Rockefeller didn't even know who Pelé was, so he called Henry Kissinger, who had become the U.S. secretary of state. Luckily, Kissinger remembered meeting

Pelé and was also a huge soccer fan. He called the Brazilian secretary of state and explained that having Pelé come to play in the United States would be "a tremendous asset for Brazilian and U.S. relations." That sealed the deal; Pelé was finally headed for America.

Pelé waves to the cameras as he enters the field for his first game as a New York Cosmo.

Hundreds of reporters packed the New York City press conference that introduced Pelé as a New York Cosmo. It signaled the start of what would be a short but intense affair between the American media and the soccer star and his new league.

"Spread the news to the world," Pelé said, in halting English but with his trademark grin. "Soccer has arrived, finally, in the USA!"

Still, soccer was a tiny sport in America in 1975 and even Pelé could not make the Cosmos or the sport instantly popular. Nor could he turn the team into champions overnight. He joined them with just a few games left in the 1975 season, and they still finished with a losing record. The attendance increased at all of Pelé's games, but the fans were mostly immigrants, people who knew of his skills from

their home countries. The mainstream American fan raised on baseball and football still had little interest. However, the American media were starting to take notice. One writer who hated soccer was Dick Young of the *New York Post*. To show Pelé what he thought was a "real" sport, he brought him to a Mets baseball game. Young was put to shame when the crowd recognized Pelé and started chanting his name; even in the heart of America's national pastime, Pelé was a superstar.

Meanwhile, on the field, Pelé was finding that life in the NASL was a far cry from the fields of Brazil. He would make perfect passes to teammates who didn't know they were coming and he played on fields that were pitiful examples of

Ross and Warner even plastered their New York City offices with advertisements for Pelé's first games.

Pelé and Dallas Tornado Kyle Rote Jr. honor each other's national flags before Pelé's first U.S. game.

soccer pitches. After his first game—in which he naturally scored a goal—he declared that he would never play at the Cosmos' Randall's Island home again because he had developed a horrible green fungus on his feet. It turned out that the less grassy parts of the shoddy field had been spray-painted green to make them look more attractive to the national TV audience (CBS aired Pelé's first game nationwide, its first-ever national soccer broadcast from inside the United States), and the "fungus" on Pelé's feet was just the paint.

Pelé had to make other adjustments, such as playing on artificial turf at some stadiums, something he never had to do in Brazil or Europe. After one game in Seattle, he told the press, "I felt like my feet were on fire. But I noticed the Seattle team used different shoes, so I will try those next time." But he took all these issues with his usual grace and calm, avoiding acting like a selfish star and trying not to let his celebrity get in the way of the team. Toward the end of the 1975 season, *Sports Illustrated* called him "a breath of fresh air in professional sports." For his part, Pelé said, "I've always been a

PITCH

A soccer field is often called a pitch, especially outside the United States.

team man. I still am. Please don't expect me to win the game alone. We must work together."

That was easier said than done. The Cosmos themselves played in awe of this soccer god. "The biggest challenge for us was not stopping during the game just to watch him play," said Cosmos defender Werner Roth.

After Pelé's first Cosmos game, *Sports Illustrated* had written: "The other Cosmos all too often seemed unprepared. It appeared that [Pelé] was not so much promoting U.S. soccer as exposing it." Exposing it, that is, for the less-than-stellar league that it was at the time.

In his first game with the Cosmos, Pelé quickly showed American fans the moves that had made him a legend.

By 1976, Pelé had led the Cosmos into giant Yankee Stadium; in this game, he got two goals and two assists.

How popular was Pelé during his time with the NASL? Attendance in the league quadrupled in his first year. One time, he was slightly injured a few days before a game in St. Louis, and the game was postponed until he was fit to play!

Following 13 games with the Cosmos in that 1975 season, during which he had helped the NASL draw bigger and bigger crowds at every stop, Pelé found himself on airplanes again: Just as Santos had done, the Cosmos were taking their show on the road, showcasing their star in Europe and the Caribbean. It was not Pelé's first choice to start traveling again, but it was a good way for him to get to know his teammates and to discover ways that they could improve. After those trips came a series of longer ones, this time for Pepsi, who in 1973 had signed Pelé and Mazzei up to put on a series of soccer clinics. In fulfilling their obligation, the two men ended up traveling to Europe, Africa, and even Japan.

Meanwhile, the marketing muscle of Warner was paying off for Pelé. He now had endorsement contracts to promote soccer balls, soccer shoes, coffee, perfume, toys, motorcycles, cars, and

soda. Though it would have earned him perhaps millions more dollars, he still refused to endorse any alcohol products (he did drink toward the end of his career, but only rarely) or tobacco products (to protect his athlete's body, he never smoked).

For Warner, the news was also good. As explained in *Once in a Lifetime*: "Steve Ross put his empire behind the idea of American soccer; he was a dream maker and a risk taker." The enormous risk he had taken by putting the Warner name behind Pelé and the Cosmos began to pay off in 1976. Due to the large crowds that wanted to see Pelé play, the Cosmos played their games that season in 56,000-seat Yankee Stadium, the most famous baseball park in the land. In addition, because Ross and Toye knew that Pelé could not win alone, they brought in more stars—starting with Italian-league top scorer Giorgio Chinaglia, the first player in

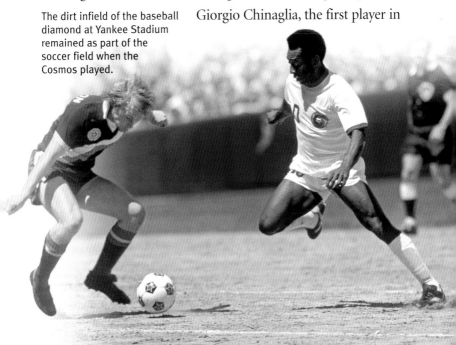

The dirt infield of the baseball diamond at Yankee Stadium remained as part of the soccer field when the Cosmos played.

the prime of his career to migrate from European soccer to the upstart American league. Then, as it does now, money talks, and Ross had the money to spend.

Before long, other NASL owners reacted by bringing in their own foreign players, most of whom were at the end of long careers, such as Portugal's Eusébio and England's Geoff Hurst and Rodney Marsh, as well as Northern Ireland's gifted but troubled George

Franz Beckenbauer

The man known as "Der Kaiser" was perhaps Germany's finest soccer player ever. His leadership and discipline helped make West Germany a World Cup champion in 1974 and a three-time European champion. Following several years in the NASL, Beckenbauer returned to coach the German national team, where in 1990, he became the first man to have both played for and coached a World Cup champion team.

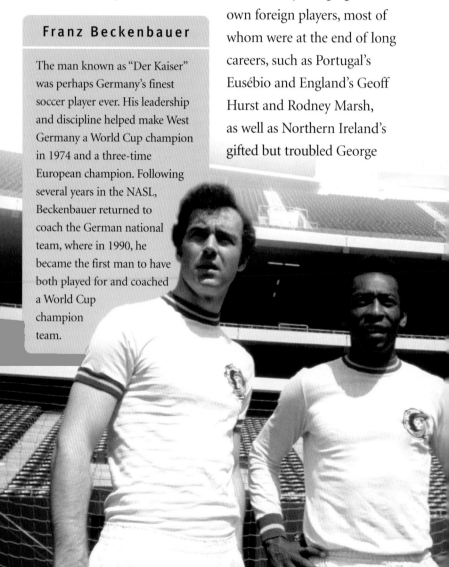

Best. The play of the league improved, and the Cosmos got better, too. They finished the 1976 season 16–8 and Chinaglia led the league in scoring. However, the Cosmos lost to Marsh's Tampa Bay Rowdies in the playoffs.

The good news, though, was that attendance was way up and the league as a whole was enjoying more popularity, almost all of it thanks to the attention given by the press to Pelé. Soon, the Cosmos would attract even more attention by signing the great German sweeper Franz Beckenbauer, early in the 1977 season. With the power up front of Pelé and Chinaglia, and the veteran defensive leadership of Beckenbauer, the Cosmos were ready to take the next step on their remarkable road. While the "soccer fever" that Pelé had ignited had helped the sport make great strides in only two years, it was his third, and final, season in America that would really cement his role as a "soccer savior."

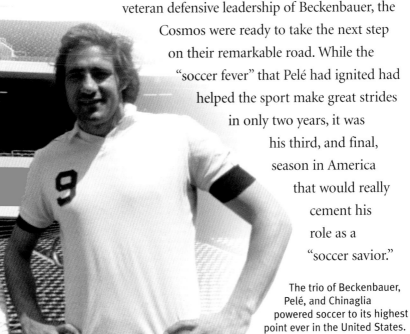

The trio of Beckenbauer, Pelé, and Chinaglia powered soccer to its highest point ever in the United States.

107

10

A Championship
and Goodbye

Few seasons in American sports can match the amazing ride the Cosmos and Pelé took in 1977. The excitement that had begun building late in the 1976 season exploded in 1977. This was especially true in New York, where the Cosmos' superstar international players found themselves a big part of the disco scene, with nights out at dance clubs as much a part of their lives as days on the soccer field. Celebrities made

Here, artist Andy Warhol chats with Pelé about a portrait he is making of the soccer star.

Cosmos games part of their visits to New York. Superstars like Elton John, Mick Jagger, and Robert Redford attended matches, brought in by Ross and his entertainment executives.

Not around to enjoy all of this was Clive Toye, who was fired before that season. Some people felt that, in addition to the goals he was scoring on the field, Italian star Chinaglia was starting to claim more control off the field as well. How much influence he had on the decisions is debated, but he did have some part in getting Toye and coach Ken Furphy let go and friend Eddie Firmani brought in to coach the team. Firmani's role, according to people who were around the team at the time, was to tell the players to pass the ball to Chinaglia as often as they could—not exactly the way to create good team spirit.

Another key change in 1977 was a move to Giants Stadium, located across the Hudson River from New York City in New Jersey. Built that year for the NFL's Giants and Jets, the enormous sports palace was much better suited for soccer than Yankee Stadium had been. Jumping in their cars to New Jersey, the crowds kept coming and growing. In June, the Cosmos set a record with more than 32,000 fans at a game, only to break it a week later with 62,319; Pelé treated the crowd to a hat trick.

Around the country, more and more games were on television, too, as part of a new contract with ABC Sports, and fans in other cities were helping to build the NASL up even faster. When the Cosmos came to town, with their traveling circus of superstars and celebrities, fans packed the stadiums.

More than 73,000 people packed Giants Stadium for this 1977 playoff game. The Cosmos won 4-1.

Between the off-field disco madness and the on-field star power, soccer had become, almost overnight, an enormous part of the American sports scene. No less an expert than famed sports broadcaster Howard Cosell said, "Soccer will perhaps someday be the biggest big league of all." The Cosmos were a meteor, a shooting star, a one-of-a-kind event and everyone wanted to get a piece.

The team came through on the field, too, winning their final eight regular-season games to finish second to the Fort Lauderdale Strikers, but then dismantling the Strikers 8-3 in the playoffs as Chinaglia scored five goals. That game was played before yet another record crowd of 77,691. It was on to the Soccer Bowl, the NASL championship. That game, Pelé's last (again!) in professional soccer, was played in a driving rainstorm in Portland, Oregon. Chinaglia scored with nine minutes to go and the Cosmos finally won it all, 2-1, over the Seattle Sounders. The Cosmos, and Pelé, were champions.

As an example of what the NASL had become—and as evidence of what would drag it down—players from 14 countries played in that game. The league was not developing enough American players to continue to attract American fans. By relying almost solely on international stars, the NASL doomed itself.

A few weeks after the Soccer Bowl, after a trip to China with the Cosmos, it was over . . . this time for good. Pelé's final game was an exhibition between the Cosmos and Santos. He would play the first half for the Cosmos and then switch teams and play his final professional soccer game for his longtime club. The game was sold out weeks in advance (75,616 would attend), covered by more than 650 reporters from around the world, and broadcast in 38 countries.

Before the game even started, Pelé created the next-to-last of his long career's most amazing moments. He took the microphone to address the crowd at Giants Stadium and fans around the world. First, he asked people to pay more attention to the world's children, and then he asked the entire stadium to say with him perhaps the only word more well-known than

In the Cosmos' bright green jersey, Pelé winds up for a shot. New York won the the NASL title in this 1977 game.

his own name: At Pelé's urging, a chant of "Love! Love! Love!" echoed through the enormous stadium.

Pelé's friends and family from around the world came to the game. His parents were there, along with Rosemari, Kelly, and Edinho. The coach who "discovered" Pelé, Waldemar de Brito, made the trip, too. At halftime, Pelé gave his Cosmos jersey to his father. After the game, his Santos jersey went to de Brito. It was, for all who attended or watched on TV, a night to remember.

Pelé shed tears when he won his first title in 1958. As shown here, more tears came when he played his last game in 1977.

The game itself was almost an afterthought. Pelé did come through one more time, scoring the final goal of his career during his first half with the Cosmos. At game's end, he was hoisted onto the shoulders of players from both of his teams. He rode out of the game a conquering hero, master of the game and ambassador to the world. And, at the same time, he was the tearful, emotional boy who had first fallen in love with soccer so many years before.

Teammates and fans alike knew they had been a part of something special. "Pelé never lost that childish sense of love for the game," said Cosmos teammate Werner Roth. "He taught me and other players so many things, not just about the game, but about life."

"His ability to communicate with anyone, even if he didn't speak their language, makes him a truly special person," said NASL opponent and top American player Kyle Rote Jr.

"I have had many great moments in my career," said Beckenbauer, "but the greatest honor was to play with Pelé."

In all, including that last one, Pelé scored 1,281 goals in 1,363 games. Only one other player—a fellow Brazilian named Arthur Friedenreich, from a much earlier era—had surpassed that total. But though he would always be thought of as an offensive machine, a goal-scoring threat whenever he touched the ball, it was Pelé's spirit that would be most remembered.

And so, the rain fell onto the artificial turf at Giants Stadium . . . and a legendary career ended.

Without Pelé, the NASL faded. Chinaglia and Beckenbauer played for a few more years, and the Cosmos won another title, but the glitter was off the stars. The NASL folded in 1984, the memories of that amazing summer of 1977 perhaps its most lasting legacy. Pelé, meanwhile, moved on to a role that only he could fill: simply being Pelé.

After playing his final game, Pelé gave his Cosmos jersey to his father, Dondinho, the man who started it all.

11

Pelé Today

With the soccer field behind him, Pelé looked ahead to his future. As he wrote in his 2006 autobiography, "Football had been my job for over twenty years, and now it was time to use the fame it had given me in a positive way." To that end, one of the first things he did was sign on with as an international goodwill ambassador for UNICEF, which aids children around the world. He has since lent his name and prestige to numerous charities around the world, most often those having to do with children, from a group that helps deaf children

Pelé continues to have a world-champion smile as he visits a Brazilian children's hospital in 2005.

CHRISTIE'S

to an organization building a new children's hospital in Brazil.

Pelé has also continued to travel the world, promoting the game, Brazil, and his many corporate partners. Pelé, as much a worldwide "brand" as Coca-Cola or McDonald's, represents dozens of companies, earning millions of dollars a year. Along with representing companies, one of the most enjoyable parts of Pelé's life after soccer has been getting involved in entertainment. He helped produce

Pelé memorabilia remains extremely popular. This Brazil jersey was sold at auction in 2002 for more than $220,000.

several albums of his favorite Brazilian music and has even composed some tunes of his own. A big movie fan, he has also acted in several films and TV shows. The example most well-known to American audiences came in 1981, in the form of a soccer movie called *Victory*. Starring Sylvester Stallone and Michael Caine, *Victory* was set during World War II. Pelé was among a dozen world soccer stars who played the roles of Allied soldiers forced to form a soccer team in a German prison camp. The movie included a chance for Pelé and others to show off their amazing soccer skills, and ended with a mass escape after the end of a thrilling game.

Pelé's role in spreading the game around the world paid off most handsomely in 1994, when, for the first time, the World

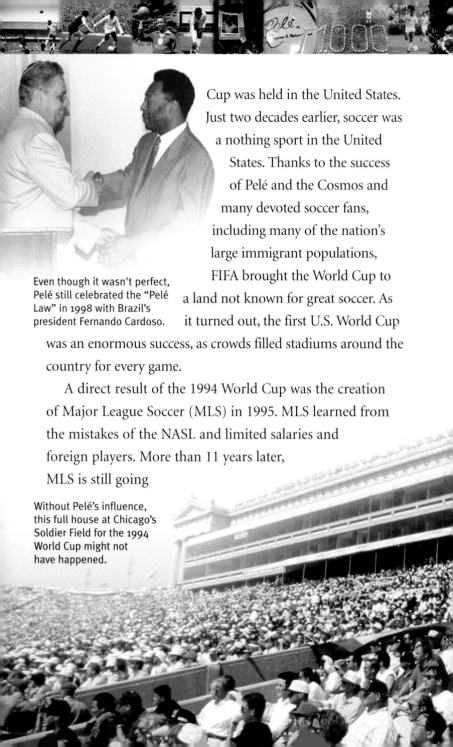

Cup was held in the United States. Just two decades earlier, soccer was a nothing sport in the United States. Thanks to the success of Pelé and the Cosmos and many devoted soccer fans, including many of the nation's large immigrant populations, FIFA brought the World Cup to a land not known for great soccer. As it turned out, the first U.S. World Cup was an enormous success, as crowds filled stadiums around the country for every game.

Even though it wasn't perfect, Pelé still celebrated the "Pelé Law" in 1998 with Brazil's president Fernando Cardoso.

A direct result of the 1994 World Cup was the creation of Major League Soccer (MLS) in 1995. MLS learned from the mistakes of the NASL and limited salaries and foreign players. More than 11 years later, MLS is still going

Without Pelé's influence, this full house at Chicago's Soldier Field for the 1994 World Cup might not have happened.

strong, focusing on building strength slowly and carefully, rather than making once-in-a-lifetime splashes like the 1977 Cosmos. However, without Pelé and the Cosmos, the American road to the World Cup and MLS would have been much harder and longer.

The fame of Pelé has even extended to the world of politics, though Pelé himself has long avoided being tied to any one party in Brazil. In 1995, however, he took on the job of minister of sports for Brazil. In that role, he finally got a chance to finish the work he and others had started in the 1970s, trying to

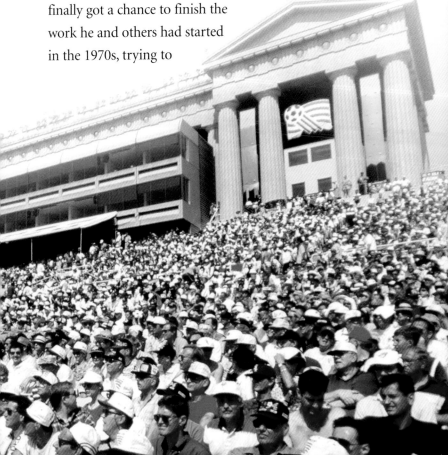

Pelé enjoys a rare moment of happiness with Edinho, whose legal troubles have been very hard on his father.

help improve the lives of Brazilian soccer players. After he lobbied for it and helped write it, the Pelé Law was enacted in 1998, freeing soccer players and other athletes in Brazil from being tied to their clubs for life. The law also tried to help fix problems with how the soccer clubs were run, and more companies are now comfortable working with the teams to promote the sport. However, so much of the law had changed by the time it was passed, Pelé said it hardly deserved to carry his name.

While Pelé's life on the field was rarely disappointing, things after he left the game have not always been goal after goal. In 1978, a week after the birth of their third child, Jennifer, Pelé and Rosemari, the former teenage sweethearts, separated and were divorced shortly thereafter. Also, it turned

out years later that Pelé had had daughters, Sandra and Flávia, with two other women he had met while married to Rosemari.

Another difficult part of Pelé's later life involves his son, Edinho, who has been in trouble with the law on several occasions. In 1992, he was convicted of manslaughter for his role in a traffic accident during an illegal car race; he spent 18 months in prison. In 1999, a judge reversed that decision and cleared Edinho—but in 2005, he was arrested again, this time on drug charges, and locked up for six months. The time he spent in jail then, two months of which were in Brazil's maximum security prison, were among the worst of Pelé's life. He tried everything to get help for Edinho. Eventually, the young man, a former professional goalie, was released until the trial, which had not happened as of the end of 2006. Complicating things, in early 2006, Edinho was charged with even more serious drug offenses and that case, too, is still ongoing.

In more joyful news, Pelé remarried in 1994 to a woman named Assiria Lemos; together they had twins named Joshua and Celeste, and Pelé remains married to her. Through all this, Pelé

Pelé married his second wife, Assiria, in 1994. The couple later had twins together, named Joshua and Celeste.

wrote in 2006, "my family are the heart of everything." He now lives with his wife and younger children in Brazil, often staying at a large farm outside São Paulo where Pelé says he is always calmest. They also have a home in São Paulo itself,

Pelé holds an oversized version of the credit card bearing a picture of his bicycle kick.

an apartment in New York City, and a home in East Hampton, New York.

Today, Pelé continues working for companies around the world, from MasterCard International, which now also sponsors World Cup events with Pelé, to Petrobras, the large Brazilian oil company. He also still acts as an international ambassador for sports, for soccer, for Brazil, and for children. "I stopped playing so many years ago, but the kids, generation after generation, still love me," he said in 1999. "It's a privilege granted by God."

Edson the man also deals constantly with the demands of also being Pelé the legend. In his 2006 book, he gives a good example of this odd mix by describing the MasterCard that he carries as part of his work. On the front is a photo of him as a young man doing a bicycle kick and it is signed with a printed "Pelé." On the back is his real name and signature:

Edson Arantes do Nascimento. Pelé writes that sometimes he wishes that he could be just plain Edson again, but he knows that as long as there are soccer fans, there will always be Pelé.

Before the 2006 World Cup, 36 years after he last played in that tournament (today, Pelé has been out of soccer longer than he was in it), Pelé's name made the top of a BBC poll as the greatest player in World Cup history. And there's still no one on the horizon who has a chance of approaching his worldwide fame.

To symbolize his permanent place in sports history, Pelé put his handprint in cement at a 2006 Los Angeles ceremony.

True, some have come close, such as the English star David Beckham, who followed in Pelé's footsteps by signing with the Los Angeles Galaxy in 2007. But as popular as Beckham is around the world, he still pales in comparison to the great Pelé, both in skill and status.

Ultimately, even if some future player reaches Pelé's height of fame, no one will ever surpass his love for the game and for people.

Love, love, love, indeed; pretty good words to end on.

Events in the Life of Pelé

1953
Pelé is asked to join the Bauru Athletic Club junior team.

1958
Pelé makes the Brazilian National Team; Brazil wins its first World Cup.

November 19, 1969
Pelé scores his 1,000th career goal during a game in the fabled Maracaña stadium.

October 23, 1940
Edson Arantes do Nascimento is born in Tres Coraçoes, Brazil.

1962
Brazil wins its second World Cup, though Pelé misses most of the games with injuries. The same year, Santos wins its first World Club championship.

1944
Pelé moves with his family to Bauru, Brazil.

1966
Pelé is married to Rosemari Cholbi; Brazil loses in the World Cup quarterfinals.

September 7, 1956
Pelé scores his first professional goal for Santos.

1955
Pelé joins the São Paulo club Santos, for whom he would play continuously until 1974.

1970
Pelé leads Brazil to its third World Cup title.

June 10, 1975
After a long negotiation, Pelé plays his first game with the New York Cosmos of the North American Soccer League.

October 1, 1977
Pelé plays his final game, spending the first half with the Cosmos and the second half with Santos.

1978
Pelé and Rosemari are divorced.

1994
Pelé marries Assiria Lemos.

July 18, 1971
Pelé plays his last game for the Brazilian national team.

2000
Pelé is voted the FIFA Player of the Century.

1995
Pelé becomes Brazil's minister of sports; he serves three years and helps create laws to help soccer players.

August 27, 1977
Pelé leads the Cosmos to the NASL championship.

October 2, 1974
Pelé marks his final game for Santos by grabbing the ball with his hands and kneeling in the center circle.

Bibliography

Books

Gifford, Clive. *The Kingfisher Encyclopedia of Soccer.* New York: Kingfisher, 2006.

Harris, Harry. *Pelé: His Life and Times.* New York: Welcome Rain, 2001.

Pelé, with Robert L. Fish. *Pelé: My Life and the Beautiful Game.* New York: Doubleday, 1977.

Pelé, with Orlando Duarte and Alex Bellos. *Pelé: The Autobiography.* New York: Simon & Schuster, 2006

DVD

Once in a Lifetime: The Incredible Story of the New York Cosmos. Miramax Films, 2006.

Works Cited

p.10: "Poverty is being robbed . . ." *Pelé: My Life and the Beautiful Game,* page 15

p.12: "with the freedom of a bird" *Pelé: My Life and the Beautiful Game,* page 17

p.13: "I just wanted to see . . ." *Pelé: My Life and the Beautiful Game,* page 18

p.19: "It was one of the most . . ." *Pelé: My Life and the Beautiful Game,* page 95

p.21: "Dico is only a baby . . ." *Pelé: My Life and the Beautiful Game,* page 108

p.24: "I felt as if I was lost . . ." "The Most Famous Athlete in the World"
    Sports Illustrated, October 24, 1966

p.29: "I've been chosen . . ." *Pelé: My Life and the Beautiful Game,* page 30

p.32: "when I found out . . ." *Pelé: My Life and the Beautiful Game,* page 32

p.41: "I was screaming . . ." *Pelé: My Life and the Beautiful Game,* page 53

p.41: "After he scored . . ." Pelé biography at http://www.fifaworldcup.com

p.48: "my best goal . . ." "The Most Famous Athlete in the World"
    Sports Illustrated, October 24, 1966

p.54: "While they protected . . ." *Pelé: My Life and the Beautiful Game,* page 168

p.54: "Watching from the stands . . ." *Pelé: My Life and the Beautiful Game,* page 170

p.58: "approached the duties. . ." "The Most Famous Athlete in the World"
    Sports Illustrated, October 24, 1966

p.63: "one of the most shameful . . ." 1966 World Cup recap video at http://www.fifaworldcup.com

p.63: "I am not sad in defeat . . ." "Rough Tactics in Cup Tourney . . ."
    The New York Times, July 25, 1966

p.65: "tripped, mauled, kneed. . ." "41,598 See Santos Win . . ."
    The New York Times, September 6, 1966

p.67: "It was impossible . . ." *Pelé: The Autobiography,* page 159

p.67: "Everywhere I went . . ." *Pelé: My Life and the Beautiful Game,* page 203

p.68: "I came to realize . . ." *Pelé: My Life and the Beautiful Game,* page 205

p.69: "Not even for all the money . . ." "Dollars Can't Persuade Pelé . . ."
    The New York Times, May 28, 1967

p.73: "Ramundini taught me . . ." *Pelé: My Life and the Beautiful Game,* page 206

p.76: "So much for myopia!" *Pelé: My Life and the Beautiful Game*, page 228

p.79: "The game itself . . ." *Pelé: My Life and the Beautiful Game*, page 235

p.81: "You can lose the championship . . ." *Pelé: My Life and the Beautiful Game*, page 242

p.82: "one of my best games . . ." *Pelé: The Autobiography*, page 186

p.85: "You need balance . . ." "Pelé: Slim Figure of Athletic Perfection,"
   The New York Times, June 10, 1975

p.88: "I had been in four . . ." *Pelé: My Life and the Beautiful Game*, page 255

p.93: "I ran with the ball . . ." *Pelé: My Life and the Beautiful Game*, page 281

p.94: "in at nine . . ." *Pelé: My Life and the Beautiful Game*, page 282

p.98: "I told Pelé . . ." *Once in a Lifetime: The Incredible Story of the New York Cosmos*

p.100: "be a tremendous asset . . ." *Once in a Lifetime: The Incredible Story of the New York Cosmos*

p.100: "Spread the news . . ." *Once in a Lifetime: The Incredible Story of the New York Cosmos*

p.102: "I felt like my feet . . ." "Yes, It'll Play in Peoria," *Sports Illustrated*, July 21, 1975

p.102: "a breath of fresh air . . ." "Yes, It'll Play in Peoria," *Sports Illustrated*, July 21, 1975

p.102: "I've always been . . ." "Yes, It'll Play in Peoria," *Sports Illustrated*, July 21, 1975

p.103 "The biggest challenge . . ." "Cheers for a Legend," *Sports Illustrated*, June 23, 1975

p.103: "The other Cosmos all too often . . ." "Cheers for a Legend," *Sports Illustrated*, June 23, 1975

p.105: "Steve Ross put his empire . . ." *Once in a Lifetime:
   The Incredible Story of the New York Cosmos*

p.110: "Soccer will perhaps . . ." *Once in a Lifetime: The Incredible Story of the New York Cosmos*

p.112: "Pelé never lost that childish . . ." *Once in a Lifetime:
   The Incredible Story of the New York Cosmos*

p.113: "His ability to communicate . . ." *Once in a Lifetime:
   The Incredible Story of the New York Cosmos*

p.113: "I have had many great . . ." *Once in a Lifetime:
   The Incredible Story of the New York Cosmos*

p.114: "Football had been my job . . ." *Pelé: The Autobiography*, page 237

p.120: "My family are the heart . . ." *Pelé: The Autobiography*, page 275

p.120: "I stopped playing so many years ago . . ." "Women's Soccer Trying to Crack a Granite Wall,"
   The New York Times, June 19, 1999

For Further Study

The official Web site of the World Cup and FIFA, the international soccer federation, contains soccer-related news stories, along with scores and rankings of teams from around the world: www.fifa.com

The International Football Hall of Fame's site features bios of current hall-of-famers (including Pelé!) and even lets you nominate and vote for players online: www.ifhof.com

This biography site provides profiles and statistics for famous players from all sports who have a Latin American background: www.latinosportslegends.com

On this site, soccer fans can find a detailed history of the New York Cosmos soccer team, along with complete game results, and even an online store: www.nycosmos.com

Index

Acknowledgments

I was lucky enough to see Pelé play once in person, in 1977, when the New York Cosmos visited the Los Angeles Aztecs at the Los Angeles Coliseum. I don't remember a lot from my youth, but I remember that day, as I watched a legend live. Soccer has been a part of my life since I was about seven years old; I still play on a team today (though we're all older than Pelé was when he retired!), and I send "cheers" to the Old Kings Road boys for helping me have so much fun on the pitch. I have also coached in AYSO for years, and I thank all the kids on our teams—especially my own players, Conor and Katie—for helping me continue to love the sport. (Thanks also to Dr. Nicholas Rose for his medical input on this book.) Thanks very much to national soccer writer Jeff Bradley, whose expertise made sure we got the story straight.

Soccer is, as Pelé said so often, a beautiful game. I hope you've enjoyed reading this story of the life of the game's greatest player. Along with learning from his amazing skills and accomplishments on the field, I hope that you are equally inspired by his personal example of positive attitude, intense effort, and love of family. Those are goals we can all shoot for, whether or not we play any sport at all.

Picture Credits

The photographs in this book are used with permission and through the courtesy of:

Alamy Ltd.: p.14 Julio Etchart; p.15 Edward Parker; p.21 Image State; pp.22-23 World Wide Picture Library; pp.23T, 24, 27, 31, 32, 37, 45, 51, 56, 57, 58, 66, 67, 74, 80, 87, 89, 92, 116-117 Popperfoto; p.26 Steve Allen Travel Photography; p.44 Jenny Matthews;p.64 Ambient Images.

AP Wide World Photos: pp.1, 11, 20-21, 53, 59, 69, 78, 84, 86, 93, 96, 97, 101, 108, 112, 115, 116T, 119, 124-125, 126-127.

Corbis: pp.6, 95.99, 100, 102, 103, 104, 105, 110, 111 George Tiedemann; pp.60, 65, 88, 98 Bettman; p.68 Wally McNamee; p.71T Leonard DeSelva; p.73 KUBA; p.114 Cesar Ferrari.

DK Images: p.10 Dave King.

Empics: pp.39, 55 Topham Picturepoint; p.43B Barbrats/Alpha; p.61 S&G/Alpha.

George Tiedemann: p.113.

Getty Images: pp.2-3, 16-17, 18, 62 Time & Life Pictures; pp.4-5, 36, 48, 82, 120, 121 AFP; pp.35, 38, 43T, 49, 72, 75, 76, 77, 79 Getty Images.

The Image Works: p.54 Topham.

Offside Sports Photography: pp.25, 28-29, 30, 33, 34, 40, 41, 47, 52, 63, 70-71B, 83, 85, 91, 94, 106-107, 118.

Rex Features: p.12.

BORDER PHOTOS: from left to right: Alamy Ltd.2006/Popperfoto; Alamy Ltd. 2006/Popperfoto; Getty Images; Alamy Ltd.2006/Popperfoto; Alamy Ltd.2006/Popperfoto; Getty Images; Getty Images; Getty Images; Alamy Ltd.2006/Popperfoto; Getty Images; Getty Images; Getty Images/Time Life Pictures; Alamy Ltd.2006/Popperfoto; Alamy Ltd.2006/Sue Cunningham Photography; Getty Images/AFP; Dorling Kindersley/Dave King; Getty Images/AFP.

About the Author

James Buckley Jr. has written more than 45 books on sports for young readers, including biographies of Muhammad Ali, Bill Bradley, Roberto Clemente, Landon Donovan, and Venus and Serena Williams, as well as several books in DK's Eyewitness series. A soccer player since the age of seven, he currently serves as the goalie on a men's team in Santa Barbara, California.

Other DK Biographies you'll enjoy:

Charles Darwin
David C. King
ISBN 978-0-7566-2554-2 paperback
ISBN 978-0-7566-2555-9 hardcover

Princess Diana
Joanne Mattern
ISBN 978-0-7566-1614-4 paperback
ISBN 978-0-7566-1613-7 hardcover

Amelia Earhart
Tanya Lee Stone
ISBN 978-0-7566-2552-8 paperback
ISBN 978-0-7566-2553-5 hardcover

Albert Einstein
Frieda Wishinsky
ISBN 978-0-7566-1247-4 paperback
ISBN 978-0-7566-1248-1 hardcover

Gandhi
Amy Pastan
ISBN 978-0-7566-2111-7 paperback
ISBN 978-0-7566-2112-4 hardcover

Harry Houdini
Vicki Cobb
ISBN 978-0-7566-1245-0 paperback
ISBN 978-0-7566-1246-7 hardcover

Helen Keller
Leslie Garrett
ISBN 978-0-7566-0339-7 paperback
ISBN 978-0-7566-0488-2 hardcover

John F. Kennedy
Howard S. Kaplan
ISBN 978-0-7566-0340-3 paperback
ISBN 978-0-7566-0489-9 hardcover

Martin Luther King, Jr.
Amy Pastan
ISBN 978-0-7566-0342-7 paperback
ISBN 978-0-7566-0491-2 hardcover

Abraham Lincoln
Tanya Lee Stone
ISBN 978-0-7566-0834-7 paperback
ISBN 978-0-7566-0833-0 hardcover

Nelson Mandela
Lenny Hort & Laaren Brown
ISBN 978-0-7566-2109-4 paperback
ISBN 978-0-7566-2110-0 hardcover

Annie Oakley
Chuck Wills
ISBN 978-0-7566-2997-7 paperback
ISBN 978-0-7566-2986-1 hardcover

Eleanor Roosevelt
Kem Knapp Sawyer
ISBN 978-0-7566-1496-6 paperback
ISBN 978-0-7566-1495-9 hardcover

George Washington
Lenny Hort
ISBN 978-0-7566-0835-4 paperback
ISBN 978-0-7566-0832-3 hardcover

Look what the critics are saying about DK Biography!

"…highly readable, worthwhile overviews for young people…" —*Booklist*

"This new series from the inimitable DK Publishing brings together the usual brilliant photography with a historian's approach to biography subjects." —*Ingram Library Services*